The Mother's Smile

"What is so simple and unpretentious as a mother smiling at her infant? And yet Esther Meek shows that this smile has momentous significance for the infant. Without receiving this smile the infant is severely deprived in its ability to believe in the goodness of its existence. In the life-giving power of the mother's smile Esther Meek discerns a whole world of truth about being human."

—**John Crosby**, Professor of Philosophy Emeritus, Franciscan University

"This is a delightful, important, and much-needed book. It is rare to find a profound academic philosopher who can communicate so clearly, and rarer still to find one who can reflect so richly on the experience of motherhood not just from the outside but from the inside. Her account in this book of what it means to be face to face, to be smiled upon, to be loved, takes us right to the heart of what it means to be human. Amidst so many threats to our common humanity this book is a timely reminder of what it is all about, what makes us who we are."

—**Malcolm Guite**, Life Fellow, Girton College, University of Cambridge

"Who knew that one could be enchanted by a book about the role of human attachment as told through the story of . . . philosophy? But indeed, with *The Mother's Smile*, Esther Meek has done just that. With clarity, humor, and humility, our guide once again demonstrates why philosophy matters so much, and that it matters early and often in our developmental journeys. Read this book and find your mind sharpened, your heart expanded, and your life transformed."

—**Curt Thompson**, MD, author of *The Soul of Desire*

"*The Mother's Smile* is rare—philosophically profound, deeply human, and poetically accessible. Esther Lightcap Meek invites us to rediscover where philosophy truly begins: in the mother's face, in the joy of being welcomed and known. With warmth and wisdom, she shows how knowing begins in delight and how the smile of the mother offers a glimpse of the face of God. A beautiful and unforgettable gift."

—**PAUL HOARD**, Associate Professor of Counseling Psychology, The Seattle School of Theology and Psychology

"This is a beautiful book of sincere gentleness and exquisite timeliness. Each page is a treasury of perfect truth from our shared depth of holy silence, words for the heart that speak to the mind. In these words and recollections, we recover the loving and gracious gaze that must accompany the intellect—the smile that changes the course of a life, that gifts us with the only self that is not lonely, the self that knows *through* love, and leads us to Christ, the great face that will not go away."

—**CAITLIN SMITH GILSON**, Professor of Philosophy, St. Vincent de Paul Regional Seminary

"If all were to go according to plan, every human would arrive in this world cradled in the warm welcome of their mother's arms, met by her shining, smiling countenance. To land here welcomed by that joyful face is the first clue to the nature of reality and the meaning of our own lives, setting both the foundation and the trajectory of existence, claims Esther Meek in this rich and delightful book. Both our origin and our destination are a face overjoyed at our arrival."

—**MATTHEW CLARK**, author of *The Well Trilogy*

The Mother's Smile

Philosophical Formation in the Welcome
of Mothers and Friends

Esther Lightcap Meek

Foreword by D. C. Schindler

CASCADE *Books* • Eugene, Oregon

THE MOTHER'S SMILE
Philosophical Formation in the Welcome of Mothers and Friends

Copyright © 2025 Esther Lightcap Meek. All rights reserved. Except for brief quotations in critical publications or reviews, no part of this book may be reproduced in any manner without prior written permission from the publisher. Write: Permissions, Wipf and Stock Publishers, 199 W. 8th Ave., Suite 3, Eugene, OR 97401.

Cascade Books
An Imprint of Wipf and Stock Publishers
199 W. 8th Ave., Suite 3
Eugene, OR 97401

www.wipfandstock.com

PAPERBACK ISBN: 979-8-3852-3647-3
HARDCOVER ISBN: 979-8-3852-3648-0
EBOOK ISBN: 979-8-3852-3649-7

Cataloguing-in-Publication data:

Names: Meek, Esther Lightcap, 1953– [author]. | Schindler, D. C. [foreword writer].

Title: The mother's smile : philosophical formation in the welcome of mothers and friends / Esther Lightcap Meek ; with a foreword by D. C. Schindler.

Description: Eugene, OR: Cascade Books, 2025 | Includes bibliographical references.

Identifiers: ISBN 979-8-3852-3647-3 (paperback) | ISBN 979-8-3852-3648-0 (hardcover) | ISBN 979-8-3852-3649-7 (ebook)

Subjects: LCSH: Motherhood—Philosophy. | Childbirth—Philosophy. | Children and philosophy. | Child psychology—Philosophy. | Knowledge, Theory of. | Personality development. | Theology.

Classification: B105.C45 M44 2025 (paperback) | B105.C45 (ebook)

VERSION NUMBER 08/18/25

Cover: "Greatest in the Kingdom." Linocut print by Ned Bustard.

All Scripture quotations, unless otherwise indicated, are taken from the Holy Bible, New International Version®, NIV®. Copyright ©1973, 1978, 1984, 2011 by Biblica, Inc.™ Used by permission of Zondervan. All rights reserved worldwide.

For Laurie!

The little child awakens to self-consciousness through being addressed by the love of his mother. Since the child in this process replies and responds to a directive that cannot in any way have come from within its own self—it would never occur to the child that it itself had produced the mother's smile—the entire paradise of reality that unfolds around the "I" stands there as an incomprehensible miracle: it is not thanks to the gracious favor of the "I" that space and the world exist, but thanks to the gracious favor of the "Thou." And if the "I" is permitted to walk upon the ground of reality and to cross the distances to reach the other, this is due to an original favor bestowed on him, something for which, *a priori*, the "I" will never find the sufficient reason in himself.

—Hans Urs von Balthasar

Thinking is not an autonomous activity, but is at its core a "being moved by an other." Because the mother's smile is a gesture of love that "welcomes" the other, her child, it does not impose itself as an opaque and indeed violent demand, but as an enabling invitation. Thus, the personal gesture that the mother addresses to the child is what gives rise to his capacity to respond in kind.

—D. C. Schindler

Contents

Foreword by D. C. Schindler | ix
Gratitude for Friends | xiii
*Pre*Face | xv

1. Dr. Philosopher Mom | 1
2. The Mother's Smile | 9
3. Face to Face | 17
4. Existence | 23
5. Knowing | 33
6. Reality | 47
7. The Other | 62
8. Friends | 70
9. The Face of God | 79
10. Delight: Your Philosophical Service | 89

Endnotes | 97
Bibliography | 103

Foreword

Hans Urs von Balthasar is known to have accorded a surprising significance to an event that he claims has largely gone unnoticed by philosophers, both because of its relative ordinariness, and because it is an experience that none of us can actually recall in any explicit detail: our awakening to ourselves in consciousness in the rays of our mother's welcoming smile. If and when philosophers address the problem of consciousness as such, they typically consider Consciousness As Such, taking for granted a fully-formed mind in operation. No doubt in part as a result, they struggle with the question of how this given thing, namely, consciousness, fits together with this other thing, the "outside world." This relation thus appears to be something that needs to be achieved or even constructed, and this appearance of course brings with it all sorts of doubts and anxieties. With his reflections on the event of "the mother's smile," Balthasar does not just give an alternative response to these philosophical questions, making his modest contribution to a discussion that has seemed to go on forever without bearing much fruit, certainly not "fruit that lasts"; instead, he dramatically shifts perspective by virtue of his entry into the original moment of what we can call the "birth" of consciousness. The child *receives* his self-consciousness; he is *invited into* reality, so to speak, through his mother's—and his father's, and siblings', and aunts', uncles', cousins', friends', even strangers'— love. The presence of the other thus coincides for the child with an affirmation of his own being as intrinsically good, true, and beauti-

Foreword

ful, and the being of the world as a gift. Just as Dante is led through the eschatological mysteries of his mentor, Virgil, and then Beatrice, and ultimately Mary, so too is the child guided by a mentor into the mysteries of the world. What he learns of the world comes with something like a personal guarantee; being, thus, has an ineluctable quality of generous self-givenness, a tone and color of love, from the very beginning.

Esther Meek is one of the rare philosophers who *has* given this natal event sustained attention. By virtue of her unique situation, she enjoys two advantages over the Swiss theologian: on the one hand, she *is* in fact a mother. Not only is she able to draw on the deep resources of an experience that we all generally have "stored" deep down within the foundations of our self-identity and sense of being, but she also has at her disposal the intimate experience from the other side, as it were. As she recounts here in various ways, she has the memories of giving birth, and indeed all of the drama of life leading up to and following from this moment of (literal) epiphany. She has witnessed her children's entry into this world as *their mother*. Meek makes clear, here, that what Balthasar refers to as the paradigmatic event of the "mother's smile"—the faithful and patient presence that one day elicits a direct expression of personality in response—is actually much more than a single event; it is an ongoing drama, unfolding not only over the course of childhood, but over the course of a whole lifetime, involving an almost infinite *dramatis personae* and a constant change of settings. Meek looks at this momentous phenomenon from a great variety of angles, each of them illuminating some new "facet" (readers will see the special importance she gives to this word) of one and the same reality.

On the other hand, Meek has also personally lived through the skeptical crisis that characterizes so much of modern philosophy—something that does not appear to have been the case with Balthasar. Indeed, she spends a significant amount of time in this book relating that experience, in order to help make clear the central importance of the natal drama. In other books (*Little Manual of Knowing*, *Longing to Know*, and so forth), she tells the

x

Foreword

tale of her "adventures in epistemology," highlighting the ideas she encountered later in life, which helped her overcome one obstacle or another that had arisen in late adolescence. In this book, by contrast, she looks backwards, before that skeptical crisis. She digs deeper, so to speak, not just to draw the outlines of a thought-process, but to relive an originary experience, an experience that she is able now, in the reflective mode of a mature, philosophizing adult, to unfold and explore, with a capacity to appreciate its significance intellectually, and to allow the wisdom of life "in the world" to shed its own light.

Though the pages that follow are filled with many anecdotes from her life, it would be wrong to see this as nothing but a personal memoir, as delightful as that would also be. Meek presents herself in this book as an example of one who has personally lived through the distinctive challenges of modernity and postmodernity, and who has found a way out, so to speak, that is open to all of us in principle. The anecdotal style reveals that the problems of philosophy are not merely "academic," as people like to say these days, but find expression in the most fundamental dimensions of the relationships that constitute our existence: with ourselves, with our family, with other people more generally, with the things of the world (the garden receives special attention in this book), and above all our relationship with God.

This observation leads to a final point: it is important not to read this book too quickly, or only once. The lightness of the style might lead one to overlook how much is going on, philosophically, "below the surface," so to speak. Because Meek has a remarkable knack for making ideas accessible without much intellectual strain—how different this is from so much philosophical writing of the last couple of centuries!—it is easy to miss the philosophical depth of the thoughts expressed in this little book. Meek seeks to show that the child's experience bears, latent within it, a whole philosophy—that is, a whole metaphysics, epistemology, anthropology, and interpretation of the world and God—and, in turn, her philosophical reflection offers itself in a form "even a child could understand." If the approach is uncommon among the scholars of philosophy today, it is something that the greatest thinkers have always been able to appreciate.

It is thus hard to imagine anyone being able to read this book without real reward: those, on the one hand, who have already studied philosophy in some depth will discover a new dimension of experience that they have probably not explored much before, and can look forward to seeing things that could very well bring about a shift in their perspective. Those, on the other hand, that are new to this way of thinking may come to see that they have been philosophers all along without having realized it, because the train of thought that Meek unfolds here in such a cheerful and friendly way will bring them irresistibly into this great mystery at the beginning of all of our lives. She shows us that the most basic philosophical act—a great Yes to being as such—is not a grand achievement reserved only for the heroes of the mind, but has always already been ours. We simply have to retrieve this original experience.

In a word, Esther Meek's *Mother's Smile* is a joyous celebration of the gift of being, reminding us that this gift is a social event that takes place in the quintessential human experience of the child's being welcomed into the world by an ambassador of Love Itself.

D. C. Schindler
Professor of Metaphysics and Anthropology,
Pontifical John Paul II Institute for Studies on Marriage
and Family at the Catholic University of America

Gratitude for Friends

In addition to my mother, Edith Lightcap, and all the faces of welcome in my life, this little book and I have received the noticing regard and helpful insights of its endorsers, along with Starr Meek Plato, Mary Lates, Alicia Crumpton, and Meg Glendening. Thanks to my editor and friend, the Rev. Dr. Robin Parry. And I'm thrilled to display the artistry of print maker Ned Bustard on this cover.

Special thanks to the Gospel Alliance of Maine, at whose Women's Breakfast I gave the talk that birthed this book. I'm glad to acknowledge a most helpful academic conversation with my colleagues at The Seattle School for Theology and Psychology, where I am Senior Scholar. Special thanks to Dr. Paul Hoard, who orchestrated that symposium and collection of essays in The Seattle School's academic journal, *The Other*.

Warmest gratitude to Dr. D. C. Schindler for his profound philosophical insight and for contributing this foreword, as well as for his friendship and solidarity in inviting the real.

Thank you all for the philosophical service you render in seeing and delighting in so many, including me and *The Mother's Smile*.

Pre*Face*

Have you witnessed the moment when a young mother first sees her newborn child? Mother is holding her infant to herself, gazing into their face in rapture, smiling a joyous, self-giving, surprise-filled, welcome. Have you witnessed Baby's first smile in response? Or seen Baby's rapture beholding Mother in early months? Have you been blessed to *be* Mother? If these haven't been firsthand experiences for you, others' photographs of these precious moments are in endless supply.

Though you don't remember it, at the outset of your own life the baby was you. Assuming ordinary circumstances, as a newborn, you were the recipient of your mother's welcoming smile—as were we all. There are exceptions, we'll note, but they serve to underscore this far more common experience.

More than physical and emotional factors are in play in the primal encounter of mother and child at birth. Philosophical ones are as well, although this philosophical service isn't one that has commonly been appreciated. In this little book, I want to make the case that you and I are formed philosophically in the rapturous welcome of our mothers. Now as adults we no longer see our mother's face through baby eyes, but philosophical formation is sustained as we see ourselves being seen in the delighted regard of certain close friends.

PreFace

I do not at all mean to exclude fathers or other family members, who carry out this philosophical ministration as well. I only mean to highlight the distinctive service of mothers in babies' earliest months, and friends throughout life. Fathers, grandparents, and other family members also serve as operative faces in our lives, our best of friends in this philosophical service; they even fill in for Mother, especially in a case of her unnatural absence after our birth. We all need to heed the message of this book. It is in the welcoming smile of mothers and friends that we receive the implicit life-shaping philosophical orientation fundamental to our entire lives.

Philosophy concerns the most fundamental matters we human persons can't help but live out responses to: who we are as persons, what life is about, what reality is, how we are involved with it in understanding and acting, and our undergirding wonder and belonging in the world. One need not have taken a philosophy course to be philosophical; one needs only to have been born a human person. We are philosophical at the very core of who we are. We live out a philosophy, often without realizing it. Philosophy, I believe, is our birthright. This is not to say that reflecting philosophically is particularly easy. It can be difficult because these fundamental matters lie so near to who we are. When we try to express them, the words we suggest must be indwelt for a while so as to grasp and employ them. But philosophy is fraught with wonder; it is joyous to probe even in half-understanding. Philosophy, it is my unwavering conviction, is meant for everyday living. Mothers and friends form and sustain us in our fundamental philosophical orientation. Our implicit philosophy in turn permeates and shapes all that we do.

> **It is in the welcoming smile of mothers and friends that we receive the implicit life-shaping philosophical orientation fundamental to our entire lives.**

PreFace

In these pages I will trace the philosophical outlook that emerges in the gaze of the loving mother and others. I hope to show why this natal philosophy holds pride of place, and why it matters as a philosophical paradigm critical in our modern age, restorative and valuable to us in everyday life, thought, and work. I want to encourage us all to reinstate the superior philosophy naturally formed in our early childhood.

Imagine for a moment, in stark contrast to the deeply natural and common delight of mother and child with each other, a horrific alternative: a child who suspects and rejects their mother's welcome, refuses to see themselves being seen. Heartbreakingly, this happens, perhaps most commonly as part of the tangled period of adolescence. It is neither original nor natural.

A philosophical version of this characterizes the modern age in which we live. The defective philosophy defining our time resembles the horrific alternative I mentioned. In effect, it rejects our primal philosophical shaping in the welcoming face of the mother.

By the modern age, or modernity, I have in mind our inherited way of thinking in the West dating from the 1600s to the present, and in important ways only growing more strident. Although it isn't our natal outlook, we seem to inhale it and live it in later years. Our modernist era, philosophically unnatural, is woebegone and toxic. The claims of this book present a timely challenge to our modern age, and they offer much needed philosophical healing.

Without the face of a mother, a baby cannot survive. Similarly, in rejecting the formative, life-shaping philosophy forged in the gaze of mothers and friends, we become philosophically deformed. The philosophical formation we receive from Mother and friends, if we return to embrace it, offers much needed philosophical healing to restore us, our philosophy, and our world to wholeness. If we are to live in harmony and shalom, effective caregivers for the world in our lives and professions, in our era, we must return philosophically to the more natural, primal version—the one forged in the mother's smile.

PreFace

I hope that this tiny treatise is big with philosophical payoff: not only is returning to embrace our natal philosophical formation personally and culturally restorative, dispelling the grip of modernity's thrall; not only does returning to this philosophical paradigm enhance and enrich our involvement with the world; not only does it restore a superior philosophy; but seeing how we are formed philosophically in the attentive regard of mothers and friends offers an on-ramp for the everyday philosophical life.

Why care to live a philosophical life—something out of vogue thanks to modernity's anti-philosophical penchant? The response is simple: *because you already are*. You are a human person: to be human *is* to be philosophical. We shape a philosophy of life that makes sense of our lives, filling it with meaning and purpose, orienting and guiding our aspirations, deepening our wonder and love, growing our wisdom and prudence. If you believe in God, that belief is profoundly of a piece with these matters—for believers, God is the most real, most desired, most loveable, beautiful, good, and true Person.

How does one become intentional in living a philosophical life? Again, the response is simple, though it unfolds over a lifetime. Start to attend to the philosophical matters already permeating and playing out in all the dimensions of your life. No one can take a single step without a philosophy of the real and our involvement with it; but it is another matter to pay attention and give thought to how it shapes our ventures. Also, notice glimmers of wonder at existence that appear and endlessly beguile us. Where in your life are you already drawn in wonder to the real, in beauty, goodness, and truth? Where are you groping toward it as toward a beckoning star? Where there is wonder, philosophizing is under way.

Cultivate and feed your philosophical attentiveness. Thinking about philosophy is already philosophizing! Live your life thoughtfully attuned to fundamental matters of our humanness, reality, and our involvement with it in knowing and action. This will also involve contemplation, reflection, reading and conversation. As part of my own philosophical journey I have tried to write books that express an everyday philosophical approach. These offer a way-in to an intentional philosophical life. I trust that this book feeds your philosophizing. Specifically as per this book, recognize that you enact responsible philosophizing as you convey delighted welcome and noticing regard as mothers and friends.

This book commissions us in philosophical service, as mothers, fathers, family, and friends, to gaze with delighted, attentive regard upon others, beginning with our tiniest children. May they see our delighted faces beholding and welcoming them. Our friends need this from us, as do our neighbors, our city, and the others, personal and otherwise, of our world. If we all live philosophically into this noticing regard for the other, the world will be a better place.

May this book's reflection deepen your gravitas as a mother or a friend. May it deepen your gratitude for your mother and your friends. May it remind you to see yourself being seen with profound regard and delight. May it deepen your sense of the dignity and reality of who you are in the world. May it heighten your commitment to offer delighted noticing regard to others.

1

Dr. Philosopher Mom

Now into my eighth decade, this little book also is a bit of a memoir. From my vantage point I reflect on the arc of my life as a philosopher and a mother. I foreground a theme that has been growing throughout my philosophical life and work.

Dr. Philosopher Mom

For decades now I have thought of myself as "Dr. Philosopher Mom." Especially when my children were tiny, I fought a palpable disconnect between my philosophical work and my parenting. I was trying to do both well, and continually feeling that each kept me from doing the other as I should. I remember coming home from teaching a class one evening, scooping up my crying baby, and thinking: she has no appreciation of what I am doing at school, and my colleagues and students have no appreciation of what I am doing at home! It seemed at that time that philosophy and parenting, like oil and water, didn't mix. At times I felt that my brain was turning to mush as I cared for my three tiny children. It is now in retrospect, from my vantage point as "Dr. Philosopher

Grandmamà," that I affirm that I was (and am) carrying out formative philosophical ministration.

Very soon I came to realize that parenting is the most philosophical profession you can have. Parents, for example, word their baby's world to them—and therein offer them the world. The wording is an eye-opening and a valuing. One of my toddlers called every flying machine she saw an airplane—until the day I said to her, "A helicopter goes wop, wop, wop." From that day on she nailed the distinction and noticed the helicopters (which were numerous there in South Louisiana). Author Walker Percy, in his essay, "Naming and Being," writes that naming opens our eyes to what is there, and celebrates it, too. Parent and child are "co-celebrants of what is."[1] This is philosophically profound.

> Over time the distressed disconnect between parenting and philosophical work transmuted into a delightful blend. I realized I had the best of both worlds.

The story of my time as a young mother and young philosopher is one of searching for a way to take philosophy, so to speak, out of the ivory tower and to the kitchen table—as I personally needed to and wanted to as I attended to my growing children. Those years grew my conviction that philosophy is for us all in the everyday. Whatever I am reading and trying to understand, I shouldn't consider myself to have finished my philosophical study until I can express my findings valuably for the people "in the streets." I came to see that philosophy concerns the everyday, rather than cerebral, abstract esoterica. Philosophy is concrete and felt, the ground beneath and within everything we are and do. It and we deserve that it be so rendered.

I was singularly inspired and aided in this mission by the philosophical proposals of premier scientist-turned-philosopher

Dr. Philosopher Mom

Michael Polanyi.[2] I found his work in time to produce a PhD dissertation on it, which I completed when I was pregnant with Child Number Two.[3] Polanyi's account about how we actually come to know—his discovery-based epistemology—proved to make good sense of how knowing works in any venture and discipline: science, work, and worship, but also everything in the kitchen and household, and my children's encounters with the world.

Over time the distressed disconnect between parenting and philosophical work transmuted into a delightful blend. I realized I had the best of both worlds. I settled into a rhythm that still feels like what I was made for: the practice of doing philosophy at home, while caring for my household. My first philosophy book, *Longing to Know: The Philosophy of Knowledge for Ordinary People*, was birthed at home, with by-then high schoolers coming and going in and beyond the household.[4] *Longing to Know* overflows with examples drawn from my home life, featuring not just my old Ford Taurus (I argue in the book that knowing God is like knowing your auto mechanic), but featuring my children. They were the ones, in just one memorable example, who pointed down to the leafy floor of the woods and said, "Look!"—which led me to the hair-raising aha! moment of spying the copperhead. I had the privilege of teaching all three of them to read and write and get going on numbers. I taught them to drive. I was paying close attention to their knowings: the classroom and music and overseas experiences they were garnering as their lives unfolded. And I came to feel that my delight in them was my paramount obligation to them.

Now as Dr. Philosopher Grandmamà I am blessed by the beaming faces of my grandchildren and try to greet them always with mine. They are important friends seeing me in my dotage. All that I say in this book about mothers and friends is the grandparent's strategic privilege and obligation as well. Young parents, though central and critical to the philosophical formation of their tiny children, generally have less leisure for extended reflection! The grandmamà post may be more suited to philosophizing.

The Mother's Smile

My Philosophical Quest

Now let me tell you how my experience as a mother intersected with unfolding philosophical thought. As I see it now, my philosophizing began with the occurrence of heartfelt puzzlements at age thirteen: How do I know that God exists? Actually, how do I know that anything exists outside my mind? How could I be sure that reality was there beyond my ideas of it? Eventually I learned that my questions were philosophical. Then once I found out that philosophy is something you can study formally, I felt bound to take up the quest. Over the years, in response to these urgent youthful philosophical concerns about knowing and reality, I have developed my own proposals. I have laid these out in a series of books. In *Longing to Know* I first applied Polanyi's proposals concerning how we go about knowing in every arena of life. Choosing one main application, I showed how this makes sense of knowing God, too.

As part of explaining how we know, Polanyi frequently remarked that in the moment of insight we make contact with reality beyond our head, as evidenced by our "unspecifiable sense of indeterminate future manifestations."[5] Since it was hope of contact with reality that I myself especially sought, his tantalizing promise was like an oasis in the desert. No other philosophers I was studying even mentioned this glaringly critical matter (also the legacy of modernist philosophy). I devoted my dissertation to this claim and have continued to savor and reflect on its implications.

I came to see that this phenomenon, this inarticulate sense of a range of future possibilities, says something key about knowing, and also about reality itself. In *Longing to Know* I expressed it this way: it's not as if reality answers your questions so much as that it explodes them. The moment of insight is less like information garnered and more like a person walking in and changing everything. More like a person . . . . And knowing is more like an interpersoned encounter. Knowing, I said in that book, is like a wedding: you promise to love, honor, and obey, and then in grace reality self-discloses. In a footnote I coined the term "covenant epistemology," and promised to explore this further in another book.[6]

Dr. Philosopher Mom

That next book was *Loving to Know: Introducing Covenant Epistemology*.[7] In modernity we inherit an implicit view of knowing as collecting information, with its damaging baggage of dichotomies, such as reason and faith, fact and value, objective and subjective, and so on. In healing challenge to this "defective default," I propose that the paradigm for knowing is the interpersoned, covenantally structured, encounter and relationship. We do not know in order to love; we love in order to know. Reality, I argued, is personlike, and so best practices in knowing take the form of inviting it, as one would another person. In knowing, we invite the real.

Covenant epistemology intertwines three strands: Polanyi's account of knowing; the notion of covenant as pledged relationship, applied to human knowing; and the idea that reality is personlike, with knowing best construed to be interpersoned, transformative encounter. Best practices of knowing, then, enact a person-honoring etiquette to invite the real.

To build my case I reflect on conversations with a handful of thinkers to make the case that knowing is mutually transformative interpersoned encounter and that the real itself is personlike: John Macmurray, Martin Buber, and James Loder, among others. It was in developing this argument that I first came to reflect on the mother's smile as philosophically formative. I extend it immediately to the noticing regard of friends, as per my own firsthand experience of this. I also develop an account of self-discovery in the noticing regard of the other. That was 2011. My 2014 *A Little Manual for Knowing*, a how-to for knowing ventures, expresses many of these insights in an abridged form.[8]

Also in 2014 I discovered that my proposals profoundly resonated with the work of philosopher D. C. Schindler and others working in the contemporary classical Christian philosophical tradition. This opened up a world of depths and possibilities to indwell and to share ever since. In the first essay of his that I read, "Surprised by Truth," Schindler expounds the insights of philosophical theologian Hans Urs von Balthasar.[9] Amazingly, these include reflection on the mother's smile. Balthasar has written memorably: "The little child awakens to self-consciousness through being addressed by the love of his mother."[10] According to Schindler, this is no aside: the mother's smile serves as the foundation of Balthasar's philosophy of knowledge.[11]

My 2023 book, *Doorway to Artistry: Attuning Your Philosophy to Enhance Your Creativity*, displays the fruit of this ongoing reflection.[12] I confess a bit shamefacedly: it was only as I wrote this book that I finally recognized that I wasn't "a baby skeptic," as I had referred to myself for decades. My odd questions came around age thirteen! Now I call it, "adolescent-onset skepticism"! This realization allowed me to see how differently I came to the world and the world came to me when I was a tiny child.

In *Doorway to Artistry*, then, I argue for a "metaphysics of childhood": there is a way of encountering the real that is natural to the tiny child, barring adverse circumstances. I argue that we can and should return to this metaphysics of childhood to restore our love of the real so critical to artistry—to everything. I argue that this rescues us from modernism's caricature of knowing and disavowal of the real. You can see that this book, *The Mother's Smile*, furthers these reflections.

A Child of Modernity

So there is an important philosophical backdrop in play throughout my story. I myself was a child of modernity. The very questions I raised at age thirteen were spawned within modernity's definitive presumptions. It turns out that my thirteen-year-old mental picture of things is the modernism-defining vision of René Descartes (d. 1650), known as the Father of Modern Philosophy. Searching for a way to anchor certain knowledge, Descartes offered a powerful picture of the knower's relation to the world. The knower himself provides an Archimedean point of certainty. The self he exalts to this absolute anchor is a solitary disembodied mind, set off from the uncertainty of a physical, external world (with the knower's body consigned to the mindless external world). This disembodied solitary mind gets referred to as the cogito, because Descartes famously aphorized: "I think therefore I am."[13] *Cogito, ergo sum.* The *cogito* contains certain (i.e., can't be false) ideas. Beginning from these, it only takes following an exact, linear, logical method to reach all truth.

But the *cogito*, the knower's disembodied, isolated mind, is cut off essentially from the rest of reality. Others beyond myself—including objects, including my own body—are preemptively suspect: we can't be sure that they are even there. Ironic: the price for certainty is the dismissal of reality. Surely this is a devil's bargain.

Key to the modern outlook is the overarching commitment to mastery and control directed toward the end of utility. Descartes' view of the real beyond me as mindless material (the single counterpart to disembodied mind) abets this agenda. It devalues it to entitle modernity's manipulative priorities. It redefines knowing as that manipulation: knowledge is knowledge insofar as it is useful. Modernity reduces knowledge to information: collectible, transferrable, commodifiable bits. It reduces things themselves to elemental components.

Descartes furnished a vision that inspires modernity. It offers a picture of "me in here and the world out there." As it turns out, just as I was experiencing it, my own mental or sense information forms a wall between the two, cutting me off from the external world. In the twentieth century, speaking of this powerful modernist vision, philosopher Ludwig Wittgenstein famously pronounced: "A picture held us captive."[14] It still does.

It was this Cartesian picture that I found in my head. I had heard it in no class and no sermon. But it seemed obvious to me. Somehow it was in the air I was breathing.

I came to see that everyone in the modern West is marked by this era's implicit outlook on knowing and the real. I needed—we all need—a positive, superior alternative vision for us to be able to escape and dispel modernity's skewed philosophical vision. The natural philosophy of our early childhood, forged in the mother's welcoming smile and sustained in the noticing regard of certain friends, supplies this desperately needed, positive, superior philosophical alternative. And it is not at all a new vision; it is our first, natal, vision. To embrace it involves not an innovation but a return. In this book I draw an analogy between modernity's skepticism and a kind of adolescent rejection of Mother's welcome and of the world her faithful gaze affords us in mutual encounter.

So it turned out that my philosophical experience as a mother teamed up with my formal philosophical inquiry and development to bring the philosophical healing that I sensed I desperately needed, and that many others need as well. The mother's smile—our primal face-to-face welcome to the world—is the very philosophical vision necessary to disarm and dispel the skewed spirit of our time, and to restore us philosophically to ourselves and to reality. And we don't need to adopt a new alternative so much as return to what was originally ours. To aid us in doing so is the purpose of this little book.

2

The Mother's Smile

Let me say a little more about the particular event I have in mind when I speak of the mother's smile.

When you were born, you were caught as you came out the chute, so to speak—caught and embraced in the arms of your mother, cradled before her rapturous (no doubt also exhausted and relieved) gaze. You were held face to face, there at the beginning, and through all your feeding and just about everything else you needed for quite a long time thereafter. And if not your birth mother, some other had to catch you and care for you. Or you simply wouldn't have survived.

Mother's gaze was one of freely offered delight and welcome. Hello! Here you are! I'm so glad you are here! We've been waiting so long for you, and your being here is endlessly wonderful. Welcome to the world! When you could get

> **Mother's gaze was one of freely offered delight and welcome. Hello! Here you are! I'm so glad you are here!**

The Mother's Smile

over yourself and your desperation a little bit, Mother's gaze was beauty itself beaming on you, permeating her holding, caring, and feeding, freely given.

I learned only recently of the delivery-room term, *en face*: birth professionals recording the wellness prospects of the newborn score them for a list of critical things, one of them being the face-to-face beholding of mother and newborn. What is measured is "the amount of time that mother and newborns spend in the '*en face*' position in the first hour postpartum, during which time contact between mother and infant is uninterrupted," according to the National Institutes of Health.[15]

The particular event I have in mind is the mother's delighted welcome, which Baby reciprocates in Baby's own gift of smiling recognition. It is the first glimpse Mother has of Baby; it is Baby's first reciprocating smile. Mother's welcoming smile stretches, most likely, to include a myriad of face-to-faces filling a season of babyhood and beyond. It matures into joyous regard.

There is something uniquely profound about the birth mother's smile for her baby. It is preceded by nine long months of gestation. Baby is within Mother—one human person within another human person. Intimate. Palpable, wordless communion. Fraught with the richest meaning. The welcome of the birth mother is uniquely a recognition of the one she has for nine months been knowing not-yet-knowingly. It is firsthand, official, we might say. But words fall short when I try to capture it.

My Experience as Mother

My picture of the mother's welcome and this primal face-to-face encounter draws primarily from my own experience. Of course I don't remember my own experience as a newborn. But I will never forget my experience as a birth mother, and as a mother ever since. Now I also cherish my experience as Grandmamà.

The birth of my first child stunned me into complete silence—rare for me, I admit. Here was this perfect little person who just got pulled out of my body (forceps delivery)! I also remember that up to that moment I had secretly prided myself that I would not be like other mothers who doted recklessly and vociferously on children. I would remain aloof, qualifying my love. Ha! I promptly and utterly lost my heart to my children. When Babies Number Two and Number Three entered the world, I greeted them with unqualified rapturous abandon.

I do remember that each time it was a sobering thing to this epistemologist that the very moment I could welcome and start to know this child I was ending knowing them intimately within my body. For me that was the post-partum sadness.

The most wonder-filled moments were their smiles back at me! As every person blessed to be a mother knows, the rapturous gaze of the mother is entirely reciprocated by the baby. The baby returns the mother's smile. The primal encounter is just that: mutual, reciprocated encounter. It seems that Baby wordlessly grasps the officialness of Mother's smile: this is my mother to whom I belong, my home, my carer, my food, my own. Baby's smile reciprocates this profound hospitality.

It is deeply wonderful to be a mother of small children, for you see yourself being seen rapturously also. I feel that my tiny children formed me more fully as myself. As my babies grew to tiny then older children, I felt as if I came into my own as a person in the world. They saw me, and I saw myself in their rapture and regard. Now as a grandmamà I know to cherish similarly the open smiles of my grandchildren.

Of course it was difficult and I was weary! I struggled not to resent their "hindrance." But in retrospect, this hardship didn't hold a candle to our delighted encounter. I quickly came to see that delight was and is my first obligation and privilege as a mother. More important than many other things I might perform or teach my children to perform, my privileged obligation is always to delight in them, to make my face shine on them with smiling welcome, to see them with delighted regard.

To be specific about my thesis in this book, it is particularly these face-to-face smiling encounters that are the event I have in mind, which set the vision of welcome and which I take to be

The Mother's Smile

philosophically formative. They are not constant, of course, but they do not need to be in order to make their philosophical mark.

Being Seen

This is something key to this formative encounter in the welcoming gaze of the mother: in her gaze, you, the child, see yourself being seen. There is a reflexivity essential to the event. One must see the expression of rapturous regard directed at oneself. If Mother's smile is a consent of welcome, Baby's return smile is their consent to being seen and welcomed. For a tiny little person, it is difficult to imagine their resisting this. For an adolescent or older person, sadly this can happen: we can block the gaze of the other. You must see yourself being seen in the gazing regard of Mother, and later, friends.

Philosophy? Psychology?

In this book I am exploring the mother's smiling welcome philosophically. Psychological matters intertwine deeply with philosophical ones. I am convinced that philosophy is concrete, bodily felt and lived. Matters commonly designated as emotional and psychological intersect with our implicit philosophical orientation. The mother-child relationship is profoundly complex one, critical to the psychological health of both over one's entire life. I believe that its psychological formativity suggests and shapes its philosophical formativity—and vice versa.

For example, psychologist James Loder's account supports my singling out the mother's smile as nascently formative philosophically. He pinpoints and underscore the gravitas of the face-to-face event. According to Loder, the newborn child intuitively seeks a center around which to integrate new activities and emerging competencies. This is a developmentally innate structure. Around three months is a shift toward the love object, a person present: the presence of a human face. The baby responds with a smile as she recognizes Mother's face. The smiling response focuses primal wholeness. The face is an interpersonal reality and a primal symbol of wholeness. Loder writes: "In the face to face interaction (whether actualized or remaining an innate potential), the child seeks a cosmic ordering, self-confirming impact from the presence of a loving other."[16] Mother's smile opens a world. That's a philosophical act.

"This primal experience of the face as actual presence and in its significance as symbolic expression provides a prototype for the convicting Presence of God," says Loder. He believes that we experience the face of God in a transforming event of God's convicting presence. The problem with even normal development is that the face goes away. We long for the face that will not go away. But, he says, the seed of the solution is sown early: the child's primal experience remains the source of hope with which development has endowed the personality.

Things Go Wrong

Of course things go wrong, incredibly tragic things, for tiny children. Mother may die in childbirth. Mother may reject her child. The child may see not a gaze of delighted regard but a gaze of shame, disgust, or lust. With no motherly gaze, studies have shown, a child may die. Our whole lives may well be a story of losing (or shunting) the gaze of regard and having it reinstated. Over our lives, our involvement with our birth mothers may become strained and difficult. A child may react protectively against unhealthy absorption or rejection. A child may refuse to consent.

However, the very fact that you and I are reading this text, thinking and communicating, connecting understandingly with the world, bears witness to the effective philosophical impact of the welcoming regard of our mothers, fathers, and other key faces in our lives. Something has gone right. In some form, your mother has seen you with delight, as have others. Every decently functioning human being, around the world, and through the ages, has been the recipient of the smiling welcome of Mother in some form or moment. It does seem that certain even momentary gestures may prevail formatively, superseding the untoward ones. The smiling face-to-face encounter is such a gesture. Perhaps it is a symbol, or an ideal. It is a paradigm. It is a vision. There is a sublime reality-filling trueness, goodness, and beauty about that glimpse which can set a life on course.

It is just the risky fragility of Mother's gaze which suggests that friends also play a critical role in notice, delight, and regard. Where our mother's gaze may have been (probably was) conflicted in early moments we do not even remember, the regard of friends seeing us proves restorative. Even if Mother's welcome had been unalloyed, we need the delighted regard of friends as we mature—in order to mature. Friends sustain and bring to maturity the regard of the other and our philosophical formation in it. Throughout your lifetime, there need to be some key faces who see you with noticing regard. Honorable mention can be accorded to spouses and grandparents, and to our teachers, especially the ones who see or saw us with a twinkle in their eye.

And, I want to add this: even things we come to know can be understood as others who see us, in the presence of which we experience noticing regard. The things we discover and come to dwell in communion with, if we will recognize this, heal and mature us philosophically.

Delight—and Training!

Of course, there is another fact about children: they need training. The philosophical riches of Mother's smiling welcome require Mother's and others' determined guidance to continue to enact. Children must be trained to take care of things. Children must be trained to respect their parents. Children must be trained in politeness and regard for others. They need to be guided into covenant faithfulness.

This years-long training can upstage the formative encounter. But we should not let it. Not only does this imbalance not make mature people; it doesn't make good philosophy. The interpersoned encounter must be focal and paradigmatic; the covenant faithfulness we grow and train serves, and receives its depth and meaning in service to the overarching communion of persons.

When it comes to mature friendships, covenant faithfulness pertains as well. Coming to be friends involves reciprocity and solidarity, learning to exercise regard and delight peculiar to this person specifically. It requires abiding faithfulness, abiding by the tacit stipulations that give the friendship its characteristic subsidiary structure.[17]

Mothers and *Friends*

Mothers and *friends* are rough, overlapping categories. It is not only birthmothers who serve as mothers; adoptive mothers, fathers, family, and friends can too. But while I believe other people may serve as mothers, there is only one original birthmother—the one who has contained and nourished the child within her body—"*pre*-face." The one whose welcome is distinctively a recognition.

Friends are others besides mothers whose faces are operative in our lives, seeing us pointedly with delighted regard. These include therapists, spiritual guides, and support groups of such persons. I actually believe that the category includes nonhuman things we come to know in encounteresque acts of discovery and insight.

The category of friends pertains especially as we mature to adulthood. And mothers can also become a certain sort of friend with respect to their grown children. Fathers' important seeing of their children may serve in either category.

Another person, the first and final Person, is God. It is God whose face the mother's smile promises. It is the face of God which finally transforms all transformations, as Loder says—spiritually, emotionally, philosophically. Over one's life, one comes to see that God's was the face there from the beginning, somehow in all the key faces along the way. It is God whose face matters above all, redeeming us and all else.

I have given birth to three daughters. I could tell you the tale of each birth! These would be stories about my experiences. But it's been my philosophical reading and reflection that has brought this shift of viewpoint to consider the *en face* encounter from the perspective of the tiny child. Put yourself with me in the cradling arms of Mother as we contemplate how her beaming countenance begins our philosophical formation.

Mother's welcome inaugurates philosophically our everyday lives in this world. I write this book to show the several ways it does so. We'll sketch how it shapes our sense of our own existence and purpose (philosophical anthropology); how it forges our orientation to and involvement with reality (metaphysics) and postures us in regard for the other (political and economic philosophy); how it forms our efforts to know (epistemology); and how it opens us to the redemptive encounter of God (theology).[18] Mother's smile supplies what we need to be philosophical beings.

3

Face to Face

The infant's encounter with Mother is face to face and flesh to flesh. It is intimate in a familial way. It consists of rapturous, delighted welcome. It involves a personal address and a surprised recognition. It is a gracious epiphany, a self-revelation. It is a dynamic event that mutually transforms.

In the face-to-face welcome of the loving other, we undergo a kind of existential change. Seer and seen do not remain the same. But this is a change to become more what we are. We come into a new world that turns out to be more our home, to which we are beckoned to belong.

To gaze on another's face as they gaze on you calls you to come forth in honesty from hiding and to step up to be present. Intimacy, I've heard it said, is "into-me-see." We incur implicit obligations to authenticity and faithfulness in this event. This is because your face and mine, face to face, is an event of gracious self-disclosure, a generous gift. Gift, as botanist Robin Wall Kimmerer affirms of plants, entails relationship and mutual obligation.[19] It is the relatedness of love.

The Mother's Smile

Martin Buber: I–You Encounter

To deepen our sense of the transforming dynamism of face-to-face encounter, let me share some ideas that have shaped my thinking. When I was first developing my proposal that all knowing is interpersonlike encounter of knower and known, I tapped the work of philosopher Martin Buber. Buber's thesis concerning I–Thou, or I–You, was widely known and popular in the first half of the twentieth century. He defined I–It and I–You as two different modes of human existence or being in the world, two manners of relating to an other.[20] I–It is a kind of third-person relatedness, obviously, contrasted to I–You, which is second person. I–It involves distant observation of objects, and information, along with one's own separate, subjective experience. I–You, by contrast, is encounter, a standing in relation to the other. It is not content so much as presence; it is beholding and address rather than observation.

In my epistemology I have found significant Buber's claim that I–You characterizes scientific discovery and the artistic act. The moment of discovery, insight, or epiphany is a face-to-face encounter, mutually transforming, to the end of communion.

To note only a couple of Buber's comments: I–It says, "This is how I am." By contrast, I–You says, "I am." In I–You encounter, he writes, "the power of exclusiveness seizes me": I–You fills everything, rather than being one among many (it)ems. In every I–You "I gaze toward the train of the eternal You," toward the I–Am of God.

"Man becomes an I through a You," says Buber. Here of course he has the mother in mind as one such I–You encounter. It might be reasonable to say that the mother's smile is the undergirding, philosophically formative I–You mode of existence. But he also has in mind any other You who addresses us. In moments of insight, the things we have discovered are Yous that address our I. Over time and many such addresses, "our I" grows to become the I of I–You: it is in the mode of I–You that we mature to full humanness and love, and we deepen our readiness to know. For while a particular I–You encounter isn't meant to last, every such encounter matures us into the I of the I–You mode of existence, and "to bring the I of I–You into all our I–Its." That's a mouthful that is worth mulling over. It calls us to cultivate face-to-face encounter as the normative mode of being and knowing in the world.

To bring Buber's insights into line with our focus here: the growth, over our lifetime, of our I to become the I of I–You is a kind of maturing into the "pregnant" beginning gift of our mother's smile. Our maturation is a fuller, lifelong return on the natal I–You.

James Loder: Four Dimensions of Humanness

We may relate Buber's proposals to those of James Loder's, a psychologist and theologian whose work I first tapped as I developed my thinking about how we know. To support his account of convictional knowing (which I mentioned previously), he identifies four developing dimensions of humanness.[21] Their development provides the underlying driving mechanism of all acts of coming to know. Coming to know is more than mere information collecting; we ride the wave of our puzzlement and need, to be greeted by a surprising welcome, a transforming insight gifted by the real.

Loder's four dimensions of humanness are the *self*, the *world*, the *void*, and the *Holy*. In general, these develop over the course of our lives. It is helpful to imagine the four dimensions as endpoints of two lines laid out in the form of a cross: the world and the ego form the horizontal line; the void marks the bottom of the vertical line, and the Holy is the top.

Our humanness involves our own selves (1), coping with the world (2)—as we commonly recognize. We try to cope, and it is good and human to do so. It is "horizontal" coping: me and the world, me and the world, day after day. But our experience of the void (3), when it appears, opens from below; it undercuts and outruns our coping. Loder defines the void as "the possibility of annihilation, the potential and eventually inevitable absence of one's being." Examples of the ingression of the void include a near-death experience, the loss of a loved one, addiction, betrayal, rejection. But the fun scare at the top of a roller coaster also counts, or a monster wave for a surfer, or even boredom. In fact, the void just is the "might not be" that is our existence. In knowing, it is our being caught in a conflict, a problem, a not yet knowing.

The void is a situation that you can't get out of without intervention from beyond. In our experiences of the void, we can react wrongly in two sorts of ways. Very often in pride we attempt to deny the void; alternatively, we make our bed in it in hopeless despair. The right response to the void is to acknowledge it, crying out, in hope, for the help from beyond that we know truthfully that we need.

Breaking into the void from beyond or above, the Holy (4) is a gracious deliverance, the coming possibility of new being. Loder writes of the fourth dimension: The Holy is "the manifest Presence of being-itself transforming and restoring human being." It graciously "recomposes the world," and "anchors us on a Rock." With the coming of the Holy we experience the welcoming presence of a new world. In knowing, a breakthrough insight is the coming possibility of new being.

It is intriguing that only one of the four is the ego—one quarter of our humanness. In order to be fully ourselves, we need much from beyond. According to Loder, it is the fully four-dimensional human who has matured to being able to give love—and thus also to be a mature knower. Linking Loder to Buber: a fully four-dimensional person is one whose I has become the I of I–You.

The void–Holy dynamic supersedes our horizontal coping with a fundamental "verticality" as an all-encompassing context. I believe that in our lives we should "live vertically," live "the

> To gaze upon a face is a transforming moment of gracious self-revelation and self-gift. In this welcoming gaze, we are forever changed—to seek the face of the other, to be more fully ourselves, to be more fully in and with the world.

void–Holy dynamic." I might not exist—but wonder of wonders, I do! This might not have happened, but it did! The void–Holy dynamic comes to expression, for example, even in the simplest "Thank you!": I might not have received this, but you graciously gave it to me! In this way we joyously dance on the void, as we might exuberantly surf a comber—or, literally, dance.

I believe that an intimate, authentic face-to-face encounter encapsulates within itself all four dimensions, and the vertical void–Holy dynamic. The rapturous welcome of the loving other is the most miraculous, gracious, generous gift. In *The Sound of Music* Captain von Trapp expresses to Maria: Here you are, standing there, loving me!—something commonly felt in such a moment. This miracle gift of the welcoming face changes our lives; it changes us into people able to reciprocate love. It catches us up into a new world to which we are welcomed to belong.

This is the infant's first experience outside the womb. The baby is literally born into four-dimensional verticality. Consider this: that baby has just undergone a most harrowing plunge into the void in the birth process. The baby's world hitherto is thrusting him out in a horrific sequence of "squeezures"! Surely this is the void! Then, to be caught and caught up in the arms and rapture of the very one who has sheltered and looked for him all along, to be welcomed to her world—surely that is the Holy, the eruption of new being, the transformational undoing of nothingness. Baby is delivered, we say! Baby is delivered into the arms and gaze of the one who makes it all what it is meant to be, in which there is belonging and rest.

Mother's smile effects transformation in the life of the tiny baby. The delighted regard of friends matures and sustains this. We become who we truly are. To gaze upon a face in the sense we are considering here can never be a passive observation and collection of information. To gaze upon a face is a transforming moment of gracious self-revelation and self-gift. In this welcoming gaze, we are forever changed—to seek the face of the other, to be more fully ourselves, to be more fully in and with the world.

The Mother's Smile

There is good reason to see the four dimensions opening up, over the course of our maturing lives, in a sequence beginning with the world and the self. But there is also good reason to suggest that the fourth dimension, the Holy, occupies a kind of priority in the mother's welcome, such that our move through the other dimensions is a developing response, a subsequent development that nevertheless presumes it. In light of the natal encounter of mother and child, we may even consider renumbering Loder's four dimensions of humanness. The Holy, the gracious possibility of new being, comes first. It comes first in time; it also holds first place in primacy. It contains all the other dimensions implicitly within it. There is perhaps a presumptive care about the Holy. A friend of mine has rightly commented: "The real doesn't want to leave us in the void, just like a loving mother doesn't want to leave her baby in tears."

The point of this book is that the event of the Holy in our natal encounter forms us philosophically, paradigmatically shaping our sense of ourselves and all our involvements with the world (the other dimensions). In light of the primacy of the Holy, subsequently to restrict humanness to the two horizontal dimensions would then appear as a decided step and inevitable slope downward toward making one's bed in the void, closing the door to the dimensions that make us our best as humans in the world. This aptly describes the proclivity of modernist presumptions about humans, knowing, and the world.

So these insights from Martin Buber and James Loder gives us a palpable sense of our face-to-face natal encounter. It gives us insight in what makes the face of the friends who see us so special. They reveal just how philosophically profound is the dynamic playing out in the event of the mother's welcome and the noticing regard of others. The intent of this little book is to work out more fully the respects in which this intimate encounter shapes our deepest philosophical orientation both to ourselves and to reality and our involvements with it, including with God.

4

Existence

The most remarkable thing about you is that you are here! Existence is an incredible thing—something never to be taken for granted. And it is a deeply though simply philosophical matter.

I have a dear son-in-law, Evan, about whom I learned, while listening to his father's wedding toast, that as a tiny child he would dress up (as a cowboy, for example), march into the room, and announce: "Here I am!" His parents had given birth to him following loss and a lengthy wait. Can you not imagine their delighted wonder whenever that little boy pranced in? Can you imagine their beaming faces?

The Wonder of Existence

Human existence is wonder-filled because you and I might not exist. We are contingent beings—that's a philosophical term that means that our existence is dependent on someone else—ultimately, on some other who isn't contingent.

The Mother's Smile

Something—someone—has come miraculously from nothing. The wonder of it is something we take for granted but shouldn't. It comes home to us afresh in certain moments. It hits us often against the backdrop of loss—as it does, I imagine, for Evan's parents. Existence is a presence where there might be absence.

The birthing of a child is the stuff of wonder itself. "Wonder of wonders! Here you are!" Even if the child has been "expected," their arrival engenders surprise and awe.

"I have been thinking about existence lately . . . ," says Reverend John Ames. In Marilynne Robinson's novel, *Gilead*, Ames is an older, terminally ill pastor writing at length to his very young son. "I suppose you're not prettier than most children. You're just a nice-looking boy, a bit slight, well scrubbed and well mannered. All that is fine, but it's your existence I love you for, mainly. Existence seems to me the most remarkable thing that could ever be imagined."[22]

How we come to sense our own existence, how well we come to grasp it, and how we live out the wonder—these are a matter of philosophical formation.

Being Seen—or Not

We shouldn't take our existence for granted, but we can have trouble sensing it as well. Believe it or not, in my travels I have talked with a young man who was not sure that he exists. This may seem ridiculous, but it begs the question: How do you and I in fact know that we exist? How do we rest in the confidence of this fundamental wonder? How do I know that I am here? That I am not just another object, but am me? And how may we live out this simple philosophical wonder, like Reverend Ames?

There are other versions of that young man's extreme. I believe that modernity spawns them. I, myself, for years lived with the feeling that I wasn't visible. I felt that I could see others all around me, but if I were to turn my eyes in the other direction, toward myself, there was "nothing there." Or I would feel that I was some kind of fortress with nothing but nothingness inside its impregnable walls. Effectively, I did not exist.

Existence

I recall one day when as an adult this weirdness began to dissipate: some graduate students invited me, their professor, to their party. I realized that my presence mattered to them. Then a few years later I published my first book. This gave me a chance to be heard (for three hundred or so pages of philosophizing), and to be seen—in a new light, yes, but most significantly, to be seen.

Another specific encounter proved to be eye-opening. In a conversation with a surprised and enthusiastic reader who was a pastor and counselor, I saw his countenance as he contemplated me. In that moment, I felt quite palpably that that empty hole of nothingness filled in, as a dentist fills a cavity in a tooth, packing the soft compound down to the very bottom. I felt that this gaze was retroactive, healing my core back to my beginning. In some way it restored me in my mother's first beholding. It healed my sense of it. I also felt myself beheld by the face of God. I had needed to be seen to sense that I was here. I needed to see and feel myself being seen with delighted regard. This experience and others are why this book marks the contribution of mothers and friends.

Reflecting on that encounter, I coined the term "noticing regard." My palpable experience of noticing regard then led me to wonder whether as a child I had not been noticed. This was not a question I had ever thought to verbalize before. I had been born into a family of grownups: my siblings were very much older. It seemed to little me that the grownups were either grandly good or grandly bad. My parents had their hands full with family drama. I presume in principle that my own parents saw me. I am sure they were doing their best with this "afterthought" of a baby. But I felt that their attention was elsewhere.

I now see that I myself might also have come to block their seeing as somehow threatening, or as something of which (wrongly) I felt I was unworthy. I realize in all humility that it takes humility to accept the gift of others—even others' gracious seeing of us. My fault may well have been pride. Or acedia—a deep-level refusal to consent to reality. More of acedia presently.

But perhaps it was simpler and earlier—at the very beginning: in those days, mothers were anesthetized generally for their births. How could this newborn have received any decent rating for *en face*? Under general anesthesia, my mother was asleep!

I came to believe that my personal experience of noticing regard or lack of it was philosophically significant. In *Loving to Know* I was making the case for covenant epistemology, showing that knowing is interpersoned and reality is personlike. I culled closely related and immensely rich ideas from several thinkers about the gaze of mothers and others, which shape our knowing and suggest a personlike reality: Elizabeth Moltmann-Wendel's thesis that touch and gaze bring us to be "at home" in our bodies; Simone Weil's notion of creative attention, akin to my notion of noticing regard; Robert Farrar Capon's pitch for the amateur—the lover— "to look the world back to grace"; John Macmurray's account of persons as persons in communion.[23] Some of these I recur to in this book.

Seeing Oneself Being Seen

But recently reading German philosopher Robert Spaemann has yielded further philosophical insight about our sense of our own existence—which he traces to the mother's smiling gaze. How does one know that one exists? Spaemann replies that it is just that I see Mother seeing me.[24] What—whom—she is recognizing and gazing on rapturously and addressing is not my body as an object, but me, my self. She is not just having her own conception (!) of me. I am not Mother's object; I am her other.

I know I exist because I see my very self, a person, mirrored in the visage of Mother and others. You may be familiar with the Mirror of Erised, in the *Harry Potter* series.[25] Harry and Ron look in the mirror, and each sees what he most desires. Of

> **How does one know that one exists? Spaemann replies that it is just that I see Mother seeing me.**

Existence

course, in that story, the mirror holds a dangerous temptation of exiting real life for a dream, and a futility of reaching that dream. "Erised" is "desire" backward. But let's adapt the example to match what we are exploring here: I—baby I—see myself mirrored in the eyes of my loving mother. I see in the mirror of her eyes that I am, that I—the real me—am here. I exist. I see Mother seeing me. What's more, welcome is a highly sophisticated interpersonal gesture of consent.

According to Spaemann, this is a central formative philosophical event.[26] Mother sees my adorable face and hands and toes; and she recognizes and addresses me. She isn't making an inference; it is a recognition of the real me within and beyond all the showings. Here you are! Spaemann says that this makes my subjectivity objective. I, a subject, a person, am *objectively here*. I am the other of another.

We need to take care here not to disconnect "the real me" from my body. Just this Cartesian disconnect lies at the root of modernity's faulty vision. But just as our formative encounter fundamentally concerns the mother's gaze and smile, it fundamentally concerns mother and child's bodied touch. Just as Mother is making my subjectivity objective, we might say, she is making my objectivity subjective. She is making it personed. As Moltmann-Wendel writes: I am my body—"though many bodies still are haunted by Descartes' remark."[27] And this is no reductivism: I am not merely my body. I do not reduce to my material components.

To employ the well-known lingo of Martin Buber, in Mother's "You," I am "I." I come to myself, as here, in the gaze of the loving other. Mother is that primal other. Spaemann writes that persons are real only in the plural, that is, as subjectivities that have become objective for one another. "My subjectivity is an objective reality—and this is what we mean by 'persons.'"[28] There can ultimately be no such thing as a singular person. We might play on this quip: It takes one to know one! More accurately here: It takes an other to know oneself, to know oneself as here.

Spaemann notes that "the number three has exemplary significance. We tend to overestimate the significance of dialogue."[29]

The Mother's Smile

But the three-fold relationship distinctively brings the essence of personhood to light. We might think of Dad as this primal third. I witness two others speaking about me.[30] A special sense of my own existence issues from this, a sense of my being "official." Indeed, this is true to my personal experience through my life: hearing, or hearing of, two others talking about me, assuming they are saying good things, makes me feel solidly here. We can extend this easily to imagine a regular large family gathering, in which a child would be seen and celebrated and commented on continually.

The gaze of the other is not a psychological crutch for a damaged identity (although it could be). And it isn't only a matter of psychological health, although it certainly is that. The gaze of the other is philosophically essential to my sense of my self as existing. My self is not its own thing first, independent of others, of which I have an inward sense in advance of being seen by others. My self as here, existing, is forged philosophically in the gaze of the loving other. "Welcome! Here you are!" We say in response: "Here I am!"

There is a paradox here, says Spaemann: I am formed to be a mature person, standing on my own, only in relationship to the other.

> The self-consciousness that allows us to distance ourselves from the way we appear to others is itself inconceivable without those very others. It is only through other persons that we learn to actualize our own personhood. Only as being recognized as someone do we acquire basic self-respect. It is only through the gaze of others that we become visible and real to ourselves.[31]

But this just reveals the dynamic of healthy love: a relatedness that enhances each person, and individuality that in turn enhances the relatedness.

A sense of our own existence—originating in Mother's smile, seconded in the relation with Dad, sustained through our lives in the noticing regard of family and friends—proves both paradigmatic and formative of our knowing, and of our sense of reality (our next two chapters). In their steady gaze of "You," says

Existence

Spaemann, "I find myself to be an objective reality that represents a standard by which to measure every true judgment."[32] Also:

> The situation in which a self-conscious subject knows himself to be the object of an other's knowledge knows that this is not a limit-case or an exception, which therefore cannot serve as a model for our relationship to reality; instead, it is the paradigm for our relationship to reality and for our normal concept of truth.[33]

Having known their own objectivity as the other's other, Baby will be doing the same thing in the opposite direction: recognizing and addressing objects as others. This begins with Baby's first responding smile. We'll see that this will be key to our philosophical involvement with the real.

Of course, Baby undertakes no explicit reasoning process. This encounter is a natural, implicit, but highly sophisticated, lively, interpersoned event, a recognition and an address. But it is fundamental to our sense of being here. That I struggled with a sense of non-existence later on in my youth, and strove to reason about it, indicated that at some point something had occurred to eclipse the primacy of this first encounter. It could well have been my own rejection of being seen by another. It could well have been modernity.

Studying this essay of Spaemann's has helped me to a surprising realization about myself, one fraught with philosophical import. I have related to you my youthful skepticism about knowing and the real. And now I have confessed my quirky feelings of nonexistence. It never occurred to me to connect these—until now. Spaemann writes:

> How do we come to attribute being to a reality beyond what the encountered object is for us and what we experience of it? Is there in turn a basis for this in the experience itself? There is indeed such a basis, and that is the communication of persons. Persons make evident to one another that they themselves are still something more than what they show of themselves.[34]

Spaemann remarks categorically: "Nothing can be real to the person who is not real to himself."[35] My feeling of my own non-existence, and my adolescent doubt of the world beyond my head, were profoundly connected. It is quite possibly because I did not feel noticed that I doubted both! Later, as I have come to feel noticed, not only my self but also the world around me has become real.

The Absent Other and the Unseen Self in Modernity

The implicit philosophical picture that defines the modern age played a part in all this. The Cartesian picture of "me in here, world out there" absolutizes the self. It purports to affirm my existence: "I think, therefore I am." But it calls into question the existence of the other who sees me—persons, places, things. Modernity disavows the welcoming other necessary for me to be seen, the other so foundational to our philosophical sensibility and sense. Inevitably it turns out in the end that we don't even have a self—as I felt as an adolescent. There is nobody home.

As reductivist, the modern vision by definition rejects the primacy of wholes, of real, existent coherences beyond and irreducible to their material fragments. "Things," or wholes, according to modernity, are not things at all, but merely their tiniest, meaningless, material, manipulable components. (You can spy the contradiction here: for there to be parts there must be a whole. . . .) In rejecting the primacy of wholes, modernity rejects the person as such a whole. And it fragments the face, its own whole, brimming with welcome. It fragments the other.

Modernity is a lonely anti-philosophy:[36] it disavows mothers and others and calls into question our very existence. But for just this reason, our being intentional to reinstate our primal philosophical formation in the rapturous gaze of mother and others dispels modernity's thrall. In mirthful subversion, for people to be here, to exist, we ourselves need to offer faces of noticing regard to children and friends.

Existence

Especially with modernity's encouragement, we all forget the miracle of our coming into being. We relegate existence to being a matter of a mere check in the box. As I expressed it at the outset of this chapter, what we are going for is "confidence in this philosophical wonder." The most astounding thing about you is that you exist. You might not exist—think of the myriads of might have beens and of might not be's that surround your birth. You might not exist—but you do. As per Loder's four-dimensional humanness, our experiences of the void can restore our sense of wonder at existence—itself the gracious inbreaking of the Holy.

Living Welcome and Wonder

In the mother's gaze, or the noticing regard issuing from the face of a friend, astonished wonder adds an essential note. It is a gaze of surprising recognition and address. Mother and Father, grandparents and siblings, all greet the child with welcome infused with the awe that this might not have happened. This child might not be, yet they have in grace come into existence. Wonder of wonders, You see me! Wonder of wonders, I might not be here—but I am!

Wonder injects into things the critical "impossible—nevertheless!" (This is Kathryn Hepburn's ringing affirmation in the old film *African Queen*. She had just survived plunging over a massive waterfall in a tiny boat.) Wonder signals the might-not-be of existence. Philosophy begins with wonder, as has been said for millennia; wonder essentially permeates philosophy. To live in wonder is living life philosophically, truthfully, and well.

In truth, every thing and event and encounter in our lives, ordinary or extraordinary, may recall us to the wonder present in our birth. We must cultivate seeing the stunning "might not be" of our existence and that of other people and things. But it began with our mother's smile of delighted welcome. Our lives began bathed in facial wonder. Facial wonder began to form us philosophically. We need to restore facial wonder to the heart of our existence and our involvement with others and things in the world. Perhaps we now need to restore it because others' rapture at our existence has subsided? Or perhaps because modernity has undermined our sense of it?

As I said, my mother was asleep! I know she was weary. I know she was preoccupied with other family members. Speaking as a parent, steadily seeing one's very own child, and seeing them with regard and delight, can seem a virtually impossible assignment to carry out. In God's generosity, there are others—family and friends. But family and friends need this philosophical injunction.

We are so much more enlightened these days about childbirth practices! However, we are not without our own (barbaric?) practices. I have in mind our continual cellphone usage. A mother primarily gazing at her phone in the presence of her baby is, I humbly suggest, a travesty; a mother, a father, a grandparent, a friend—this is massively widespread. May we not discern a link between the devices of modernism and how modernism re-forms and de-forms us? Between modernism and our studied indifference to the wonder of existence?

We do not need the help of cell phones to fail to behold, attend, delight, notice with regard. We need no help to be prone to inattention, to fail to notice and regard. We need something like determined repentance, whatever the vice. But we do not need to dwell on blame. We do need to take this to heart, to grow our faithfulness to see others, to allow then to see themselves in our gaze. This is fundamentally critical philosophical ministration, ours to carry out at every turn.

To say, "I am here," "You are here": it may seem small and laughable, but it isn't. It is the richest, most profound philosophical affirmation. It brims with astonishment. It is our philosophical birthright, garnered in the gaze of Mother and others. It can take courage, responsible resolve to hold to it and live it out. But to do so is to show up in welcome and noble courtesy in the world.

5

Knowing

The matter of how it is that we go about knowing whatever it is we know is something we live out more than reflect on. That's as it should be. That's how it is that our philosophy permeates our lives. The problem is that our lived philosophy can be partially mistaken, in need of "philosophical therapy." This is the sort of distortion that the implicit presumptions of our modern age, tacitly adopted beyond childhood, introduce into our outlook.

How We Know: The Modernist Paradigm and the Maternal Paradigm

Epistemology is the philosophical study of how we know. We human persons undertake knowing in every corner of our lives: it just is our involvement in all our efforts to understand our world. Knowing is making sense of the world. In the course of living my life, for example, I attend to my family, my home and garden, my neighborhood, my town, my heritage, my calling, my church, my faith, in faithful care, seeking to grow in understanding. As a philosopher and author, writing is my professional act of coming to

The Mother's Smile

know. Writing is for me my main practice of thinking and discovery. As we consider knowing, do reflect on your own knowing ventures.

As you could see from my personal philosophical quest, my adolescent issues were epistemological: How do I know whatever it is I know? I asked doubtfully; I had no proof, I felt, for something I needed fundamentally: knowing God, not to mention knowing the rest of reality. It turned out that these doubts stemmed at least in part from the very modernist mindset that we implicitly imbibe. I was "in here"; so-called objects of my knowledge were "out there." I could not get outside my own head. This is just the Cartesian modernist picture which has held us captive. The fact that my quest began, at thirteen, with skepticism about contact with reality, the fact that it has taken years for me to develop—to return to—the glaringly obvious shape of knowing into which I and you were born, evidences the pervasive power of modernism's epistemic distortion.

> The mother's smile, our encounter with her in that natal welcome, offers a superior, alternative epistemology. It offers the "alternative" that was ours by birthright from the beginning.

In line with its own pervasive agnosticism regarding what is actually there beyond our knowing, our modernist outlook presumes that knowledge is mere information, information that we amass to the end of utility. We live in an age of information. We imagine it as pieces, disconnected from each other and from the world; we're ambivalent regarding whether it is disconnected from us or not. We privilege the disconnect so that we can be objective, so we think.

There's nothing wrong with amassing information. There is everything wrong with setting up "piece-y," focal, explicit information as the philosophical paradigm of knowledge. But most of us hesitate to move away from this modern knowledge-as-information

Knowing

mindset precisely because the mindset presumes that there is no viable alternative. Knowledge is information, or we do not have knowledge—we presume. Besides, information works, and that's what matters, so we say.

But the mother's smile, our encounter with her in that natal welcome, offers a superior, alternative epistemology. It offers the "alternative" that was ours by birthright from the beginning and that persists in underlying our knowing, despite the modern age's incoherent effort to eclipse it. A knowledge-as-information philosophical paradigm turns its back on our primal philosophical formation in our encounter with our mother's smile. To reject this maternal paradigm to embrace passive information collecting as a model is wrongheaded philosophically and damaging to ourselves and the world. Choosing to return to it healingly subverts modernity's epistemic distortion. It reconnects us profoundly to ourselves and to the world. It restores us to the thing we human persons are meant for: we are meant for lively, unfolding, communion with the real.

The delighted welcome in the mother's gaze forms us philosophically in our involvement with the world. As Robert Spaemann notes, the tiny child's knowing himself to be the other for an other, is "the paradigmatic case, which reveals what knowledge in general is." It is not an exception but rather "the model for our relation to reality, for our normal concept of truth."[37]

From the very beginning of our lives we are formed in the paradigm of knowing as covenanted, intimate encounter and relational communion. Barring egregious hazards, every person's most original and pervasive orientation to the world is interpersonal. Knowing, in its fullest expression, is interpersoned encounter with a personlike real. To the extent that we know, speak, think, and work at all, in some measure we continue to rely on our natal philosophical formation. The dynamic of our original philosophical paradigm is in play whenever we are knowing well: in gardening, entrepreneurship, scientific discovery, playing baseball.

It's astounding: you and I were born into enacting the most sophisticated (and true to life) paradigm of knowing that there

The Mother's Smile

is. And babies get it and are exemplary at it. We didn't have to work up to it, from passive information collecting, for example. I shouldn't have had to take decades of study to figure it out and return to it. It shouldn't be the case that our dominating milieu is blind to it. If it is, it is because it rejected it.

My Personal Quest and Return

With the particular guidance of philosopher and scientist Michael Polanyi, over the years I was working out a responsible account of knowing. I began to attend to what we are actually doing when we come to know. I also listened to others such as Annie Dillard, Parker Palmer, and Lesslie Newbigin, all of whom reflected on knowing and suggested something other than a modernist approach, a more fundamentally personed one.[38] I came to develop this covenant epistemology. It was only on the way to this, I humbly admit, that I came to the mother's smile. It was a personal discovery, something new; but in truth it was a return.

To show that knowing is "interpersoned," at the time I tapped the insights of philosopher John Macmurray. Macmurray begins his book *Persons in Relation* with the claim, "The fundamental unit of human existence is not I, but rather You and I."[39] Macmurray writes: "We are persons not by individual right, but in virtue of our relation to one another. The personal is constituted by personal relatedness." The fundamental shape of humanness, Macmurray argues, is not substances with attributes, rational animals, but persons in relation.

At first, I resisted this notion! I felt that it directly contradicted what at the time I thought was obvious—that I, as a solitary individual, am my own fundamental unit of human existence. I felt that to think otherwise would be just the sort of immature succumbing to peer pressure against which I had been warned. Of course, there is a defective, unhealthy version of relatedness that we must avoid. But this version isn't (or shouldn't have been) the original. It is the original that is philosophically formative. My initial resistance grew out of the faulty views of modernity, which I

Knowing

had implicitly imbibed—ones that were surfacing in adolescence, in my school years.

Macmurray then reflects philosophically on the mother and child—this is the title of his first chapter! The child's first knowing is knowing Mother. Baby's first smile signals this first knowing. This shapes the structure of all our knowing, from then on, as intimate, relationed encounter with what Macmurray calls the personal other. He writes: "The first knowledge, then, is knowledge of the personal Other—the Other with whom I am in communication, who responds to my cry and cares for me. This is the starting point of all knowledge and is presupposed at every stage of its subsequent development. . . . The knowledge of the Other is the absolute presupposition of all knowledge."[40]

So in my unfolding personal philosophy, Macmurray's mother and child chapter first offered a natal anchor and shaping to covenant epistemology. It is my agenda here to underscore this and develop it more fully in light of others' contributions. In recent years I have found other thinkers who take the mother's smile to be philosophically key: Hans Urs von Balthasar, especially as expounded by D. C. Schindler, and Robert Spaemann (presented in translation also by Schindler).

Features of Knowing on the Formative Maternal Paradigm

Here is a list of intertwined, defining features of knowing that I draw from their work, but that affirm and amplify covenant epistemology as I have crafted it elsewhere. These features evidently pertain first of all in the mother's philosophically formative smiling welcome. From there, and as a result, they shape all our lifelong efforts to understand reality—especially as we attune our philosophy to them.

It makes great sense to allow the dramatic event of natal encounter to suggest important features of human knowing at its best. The maternal paradigm shows how best go about our efforts to understand the world. As you reflect on these features, see if they come to expression in your own experiences of knowing.

First, knowledge is *not information but rather encounter*—as we have been saying. It isn't a passive transfer of items but rather an interpersoned event. Face-to-face encounter is for all of us our first knowing. Schindler defines knowledge as "an event of personal presence," an intimate encounter with reality, which is our other.[41] We have noted that Schindler relates the memorable claim of Balthasar: "The little child awakens to self-consciousness through being addressed by the love of his mother." Schindler remarks that Balthasar rightly anchors his entire epistemology in the event of the tiny child's encounter with their mother. "Balthasar roots our contact with the world in a more fundamental 'contact,' one that gives everything else a particular coloring: namely, the mother's smile."[42] This is the claim that we are drawing out in this book.

It is not that information isn't involved in the event of knowing. But within that event any information must be indwelt, lived from skillfully and artfully in a manner that invites reality's gracious self-disclosure. It is okay to focally identify and temporarily itemize information in order to deepen the virtuosity of our indwelt grasp. We may do this to enhance our process going forward. But *encounter*, not information, affords the overarching epistemic paradigm. Apart from the event of encounter, information doesn't itself add up or make sense. Knowing is fundamentally not knowing data but rather knowing in communion with an other whom we seek to know.

Second, the real is *not object but other*. I—my self—am the arbiter of my knowing: this is the Cartesian picture. Modernity's picture of knowledge is *"ego*logical," says Schindler: it exalts the self in knowledge.[43] In necessarily related moves, modernist epistemology exalts the self to arbiter and reduces the other to object.

According to Spaemann, when modern philosophy speaks of "the object of knowledge," technically it refers not to the thing beyond my knowing it but to my own mental contents—the mental "object" to which I attend in my knowing.[44] Modernist epistemology's object is only the object for me.

Knowing

In exalting the self, modernist epistemology becomes ambivalent about the object. Is the object inside my knowing, or there outside my knowing? Either way, the object is for me. Reality beyond me, if it is there, is something over which I am arbiter. In its mastery-motivated objectifying, the modern outlook further reduces even the somethings to their tiniest components, effectively disavowing even the things themselves. The project of modernity, Spaemann writes, is "the progressive mastery of nature through the despotic objectification of nature."[45]

Spaemann insists that "a fundamental challenge to the consciousness of the age must be proposed." Hear the telling reference to the personal in his next comment: "We need to rethink the concept of mastery, and moreover, to attribute something like selfhood to other entities simply as partners able to dialogue with Homo Sapiens at various levels."[46] To do this rethinking is to restore the object to other. In healthy knowing, the defective and damaging dynamic of mastery and objectifying observation get replaced by encounter and communion, the far more three-dimensional objectivity only possible between persons as others.

"Attributing something like selfhood to other entities as partners able to dialogue" describes our original natal philosophy, forged in the mother's smile. The other in mother, we might say, accords primacy to the other in matters of knowing and reality. The other that we know takes its cue from our mothers: not a what but a who, showing up to address (and dress!) me in welcome, an on-its-own thing beyond me, with lively depths and possibilities, worthy of my regard, there for my knowing in encounter and communion. Spaemann writes that acknowledging the reality of the other "is the highest form of spiritual activity, self-transcendence."[47] This means that in our earliest existence as baby human persons we are carrying out the highest form of spiritual activity!

So let us replace the modernist designation *"object* of knowledge" with the *"other* of knowledge." We do this as we restore the philosophy of our earliest childhood.

In our encounter with the real, knowing is *first of all receptive*.[48] Schindler writes that from the perspective of knowing as

The Mother's Smile

encounter—what he calls knowing as a drama, "thinking is not an autonomous activity, but is at its core a 'being moved by an other.'"[49] Schindler writes: "Because the mother's smile is a gesture of love that 'welcomes' the other, her child, it does not impose itself as an opaque and indeed violent demand, but as an enabling invitation."[50] Thus, "the personal gesture that the mother addresses to the child is what gives rise to his capacity to respond in kind."

It is not I but the other who initiates, self-disclosing graciously in hospitable welcome, and in the event also attunes us to respond. In my book *Doorway to Artistry* I draw out Schindler's account to claim that reality welcomes: the event of beauty is the gracious self-showing of the real that catches our attention. The beauteous self-disclosive overture of the real actually forms us to respond appropriately in kind, in love and self-giving.

In his scholarly work on Plato's *Republic*, Schindler pinpoints the question of knowledge, intelligibility, and truth. The question is whether there is reality beyond our relative perception of it. Indeed, this was precisely my adolescent question. Schindler also pinpoints the response, which he argues is the witness of this famous ancient dialogue. Knowing contains a movement of striving that is interrupted by a dramatic reversal: the real itself breaks in.[51] The real shows up and addresses us.

Knowing is first receptive of the other, but *we the knowers are involved*. Since reality showing up has primacy, knowing is our reciprocation. We reciprocate and respond to welcome the other's overture. Spaemann writes: "It is false to think that something is more adequately known the more passive the knower is. . . . I cannot hope to approach the essence of another human being if I invest nothing of myself."[52] Knowing will bear traces of the knower, a very personal kind of knowledge. "But knowledge of reality can come in no other way." You may remember that Polanyi's philosophical *magnum opus* is titled, *Personal Knowledge;* Polanyi joins Spaemann to argue that all knowing is, and is best seen to be, personal knowledge.

According to Schindler, "the fundamental act of reason cannot simply be a passive taking in; instead, it is, so to speak,

Knowing

a 'going out to meet' being."[53] The act will necessarily include "other-directedness," a movement beyond. Schindler claims that *knowing is ecstatic*: out beyond ourselves, in and with the other. In its very essence and structure, "reason is always already out beyond itself—and so in and with the other—from the beginning. As natively ecstatic, reason always exceeds explicit consciousness."[54] Knowing is a reaching beyond where we are, to be with and within an other. These rich phrases converge with the account of knowing I have drawn from Michael Polanyi's work: all knowing is from-to, and beyond.[55]

Schindler continues: "This means that we do not 'begin' our reasoning from a position outside of things, and gradually by degrees make our way toward them. Instead, conceived ecstatically, reason is already, from the beginning, at the destination of this path: it begins its activity already from within the beings it encounters, and indeed, as profoundly intimate with beings as it is possible to be."[56]

Thus, knowing also is *empathetic*. It is a "feeling in"—indwelling, as Michael Polanyi stressed. It is a "feeling with"—the etymological meaning of "con-sent." Empathy, Schindler remarks, "is not an extreme achievement of an otherwise self-preoccupied being, but the natural structure of our knowing."[57]

At the same time, knowing is *nonpossessive*.[58] According to modernity's way of thinking, knowledge, to be knowledge, must exhaustively state (from the bottom up) what it's about. The known must be completely possessed by the knower; it must be taken entirely inside the knower to comprehend it. Knowledge as possessive imposes itself upon the real. Thus, "to conceptualize is to dominate," Schindler explains.[59] Schindler argues that modernity's penchant is totalizing information. Modernity has presumed that totalizing information is the essence of reason. This view is handy for a milieu aspiring to master and control nature!

Late- and post-moderns rightly sense this objectifying offense. But since often people fail to challenge the model of knowledge presumed herein, in order to avoid the offense they choose to discredit the idea of knowledge itself. But, Schindler writes, "the inclination knowledge has tended to evince toward mastery is due, not to the essential nature of knowing, but specifically to its fallen modernist form."[60] Knowing doesn't damage reality; the modernist knowledge-as-information paradigm damages reality.

Authentic knowing does not reduce what we know to an object that we wholly possess. It is possible to know something without simply subordinating it to oneself. "One enters into knowledge and so one need not keep it nervously for oneself."[61] Not only is it possible for knowledge to be nonpossessive; it is necessary.

Knowing as nonpossessive preserves the abiding otherness, the freedom and dignity, of the other. Schindler writes this as he reflects on the mother's welcoming address; the mother, in turn, welcomes her child's address in kind—she does not welcome possession. Says Schindler: "The act of knowledge is itself, in its very structure, a generous act." I love what he says next: thus, "to know is a very precise, indeed perhaps the most profound, way to love."[62]

So: the essential structure of knowing is *a structure of love*. Speaking of the mother's smile, Schindler writes that this natal encounter is a generous gift of love, which "brings to fulfillment what reason is in its most profound and original form: a generously appropriating encounter with its other."[63] All that we have said and shown so far about knowing and about the philosophically formative encounter with Mother is only possible and only makes sense if love is the structure. We must love in order to know.

As I wrote in connection with covenant epistemology, reality is personlike, and knowing at its best behaves accordingly.[64] We must not demand, but rather, in response to the real's welcome, reciprocate to invite the real. We practice a kind of "epistemological etiquette." We love and pledge in order to know. We compose ourselves to presence. We comport ourselves in respect, humility, patience, and fidelity. We position ourselves where the real is likely to reveal itself. We live life on the terms of the yet to be known. We cultivate a dancing overture and response with it. As I wrote in connection with artistry, reality as personlike invites us first.[65] The real hospitably welcomes, and we should reciprocate in kind,

Knowing

exercising a noble courtesy to our nobly courteous host. Mother sets the tone of this noble courtesy.

Knowing is *communion, not correctness*. Knowing features a familial intimacy, a conviviality in relationship, a mutual indwelling. Schindler writes that to desire knowledge is, by definition, to desire intimacy with the world. Knowing "has a certain intimacy with reality, or rather is a certain intimacy with reality: to understand is to read the interior of things."[66] Again—Mother, and our natal encounter with her.

And this desire is fundamental to our humanness. We were made for this contact, agrees Schindler. Human persons are "ordered to [designed for] communion with reality"—knowing and cultivating it.[67] "When we know something different from ourselves we are therefore in ontological communion in some genuine way with that other."[68]

We must be sure to mark another feature of knowing which we must see to permeate all the others, and which the welcome of mother's smile expresses: *delight*. Schindler's term, quite often, is *rapture*. Hear David Bentley Hart's memorable pronouncement: "Delight is the premise of any sound epistemology."[69] Apart from delight, themes such as love and communion and empathy and welcome can sound a bit joyless, almost a burden to bear. But if this were true, they would not be the traits of knowing that Schindler and I are endeavoring to describe. Delight brings distinct and necessary flavor to all these other wonderful features. There is something uncontrived and even helpless about delight. It is response. It suggests a bit of nonpossessive distance.

Finally, *knowing is of the whole*, Schindler writes.[70] What does this mean? Why is it significant? What does it have to do with knowing as formed in the mother's smile?

Schindler's "of the whole" connects profoundly with the approach to knowing that I learned from Michael Polanyi and presume in my work. Polanyi the premier discoverer recognized that making a discovery involves shaping or spying a coherent pattern, a whole—a Gestalt—that is irreducible to its parts and to all the clues we have indwelled anticipatively as we have scrabbled toward

The Mother's Smile

it. He called this "subsidiary focal integration," for we indwell the clues and parts, subsidiarily attending and integrating from them to the transforming coherence.[71] All knowing has this structure. Just one everyday example is riding a bike: subsidiarily indwelling clues within the focal performance of biking. Your essential felt sense of balance is a great example of subsidiary awareness. Also, that coherent whole brims with future possibilities that you can only sense, not name, in that moment. Biking, for example, opens up possible paths and places you can go! Balthasar describes this whole as "concrete, brimming, a visible manifestation of nonappearing depths, an intelligible, irreducible unity."[72] There is a primacy to the whole, to the integrative pattern that coalesces in our moment of insight.

There is a kind of face to face about knowing. If you remember any experience of a breakthrough of insight, you felt in that moment that you are eye to eye with the real, which has allowed you to unearth it. That irreducibly coherent integrative pattern—that Gestalt—well, it's a kind of *face*. It is the thing that the thing is, standing there before you, gazing at you.

But indeed the whole—the integrative pattern, as a physiognomy, a face—is just what is going on in the mother's smile. The whole scoops up all that has gone before and overflows with more that is to come. It is concentrated with the deepest meaning—for you. If the mother's smile norms and forms our knowing, knowing is structured to be of the whole. Knowing the whole, we might say playfully, is *knowing face first*—perhaps like a dive into a pool!

The act of coming to know, as per Polanyi's account, involves surprising recognition. When reality shows up in the breakthrough of insight, you recognize it, but also it manages to surprise you. In this the unfolding knowing venture is like a drama—a dramatic reversal, Schindler argues.[73] The play hints at a culmination; but when it comes, the climax both fulfills what we anticipated and does so in a way we did not anticipate. "So! It is You!"—thus Buber describes the poet Goethe's encounter with a rose.[74] These words are spoken first by Mother to her infant, setting the pattern of surprising pattern recognition in knowing.

Knowing

It's just because knowing is face first that knowing brims with loved mystery—what Schindler calls "luminous mystery"—and thus is true to the real.[75] It's because knowing is of the whole, in the sense of the mother's smile, that knowing can be both of the whole and at the same time preserve and honor the "abiding otherness," freedom, and dignity of the other.[76]

Consider how starkly modernity's presumption about knowledge contrasts with the fundamental philosophical shaping that is ours in the arms of our delighted mother! Descartes, in his era-defining vision of knowledge, seems to have forgotten his mother. Sadly, his mother died when he was very small. How might the modern legacy of thought and culture that we inherit have been different had she not died? In a way, we moderns all suffer from Descartes' own maternal loss. Playfully, we might say that Descartes' famously exalted "I think" ought to be replaced with, "So! It is You!" Or, "There you are! Here I am!" May we not winsomely subvert modernity's solitary, oppositional mindset, in our lives and in our work, by being intentional to enact the philosophical paradigm that shaped us in our birthing?

Our Best Knowings

And does not this account make better sense of our best knowings? Of course I collect information about my garden. But information collecting falls far short as a paradigm of what I am actually doing as I am involved understandingly with the beds, the flowers, the grass, the trees, attending season in and season out to these things I care for, overturing and responding in a dance over the years of my stewardship of this patch of the earth. My garden is other, not object. It and I are face to face in communion. We aren't opponents, we are family. I listen to it; I am involved with it. It thrives in my delighted attention; I thrive in this communion as I indwell it with empathy. My garden is a whole, irreducible to the clues and parts, though flooding them with their proper significance, ever overflowing with possibilities, a luminous, loved mystery. This is knowing *a la* the mother's smile. It is communion with the real.

The Mother's Smile

Thus it is that the delighted gaze of our mother, our father, our family, and our friends forms us in healthy knowing. We can be intentional about our knowing to discern and emphasize these key features that flow from this primal welcome. In so doing, we fulfill the meaning of our existence, we restore our natural philosophical orientation to the world, we become better knowers, and we bring healing to our time.

6

Reality

Reality and knowing are philosophically inseparable. What you say about the one bears on what you say about the other. But we still distinguish them, don't we? In this chapter we see how the mother's welcoming encounter shapes reality as well as our knowing of it. The study of how we know is called epistemology; "ontology" and "metaphysics" refer to the study of what reality is.

Here is the text that is centrally formative to this book, especially for this chapter. These are the opening sentences of Hans Urs von Balthasar's essay on comparative religion, "Movement Toward God."

> The little child awakens to self-consciousness through being addressed by the love of his mother. Since the child in this process replies and responds to a directive that cannot in any way have come from within its own self—it would never occur to the child that it itself had produced the mother's smile—the entire paradise of reality that unfolds around the "I" stands there as an incomprehensible miracle: it is not thanks to the gracious favor of the "I" that space and the world exist, but thanks to the gracious favor of the "Thou." And if the "I" is permitted to walk

upon the ground of reality and to cross the distances to reach the other, this is due to an original favor bestowed on him, something for which, a priori, the "I" will never find the sufficient reason in himself.[77]

As we have noted, D. C. Schindler remarks that this simple claim about the mother's smile serves as the foundation of Balthasar's epistemology. This passage has everything to do with reality as well. Schindler continues: Mother "welcomes him literally into the world, that is, into reality more generally."[78] The child's first experience of both self and world in his mother's embrace is simultaneously personal *and* metaphysical—it concerns the nature of reality. "From the beginning—a beginning that is never more to be left behind—being [the real] has a personal face, and the personal always has an ontological depth." Mother's welcome inaugurates Baby's grasp of reality itself.

My personal philosophical questions expressed doubt concerning reality beyond my head. I had no proof that the real was there, and surely this proof was the most needed thing. For decades I represented myself as "a baby skeptic." Only with the writing of my 2023 book, *Doorway to Artistry*, did I realize that this skepticism did not begin in babyhood; rather, it was "adolescent-onset." When I actually looked more closely, it wasn't skepticism that had characterized my babyhood philosophically. My earliest outlook was joyous love of the real.

> The entire paradise of reality that unfolds around the "I" stands there as an incomprehensible miracle: it is not thanks to the gracious favor of the "I" that space and the world exist, but thanks to the gracious favor of the "Thou."
>
> Hans Urs von Balthasar

Reality

This realization freed me to recall my rapturous babyhood loves and their proper philosophical import. I had (still have) a 1949 children's book called *Tuttle*, about a little truck in the city of Philadelphia, where I grew up.[79] The simple line drawings depict all the buildings leaning over and calling, "Hello!" to Tuttle as he speeds happily over the cobblestones. Indeed, my "friends," as I called them, included oil tanks and street sweepers, the "El" (short for the elevated commuter train on the track up over the street) and "Billy Penn" (as Philadelphians refer to him) atop City Hall—also featured in Tuttle. My loves included the ocean a couple hours away, promised in the sand appearing at the edges of the roads, which I excitedly watched for as we sped from the city across New Jersey to the shore. Indeed, the back of my head is flat, for from infancy I would not be denied seeing! To this day I keep my nose to the windowpane.

My very young childhood, when I recalled it properly, displayed an exuberant philosophy of the real. The problem was that I had drawn back from it. I now see this as the adverse impact, not of maturing to adulthood, but of succumbing to modernity's skewed philosophy. In our lives, we seem to acquire the modernist outlook later on from childhood, quite possibly with our formal education. It eclipses our baby delight in reality's welcome. In a way, it calls into question our mother.

I now pose that we have a natural metaphysics of childhood that predates our modern mindset. There is an approach to the real that is ours naturally by virtue of our birth into mother's embrace, and operative evidently in our early months and years. This is the philosophy of the real that I have finally come around to trust and commend. I recommend that we return to it.

G. K. Chesterton is widely known for his own critique of modernity in the early twentieth century. As he grew up, he found himself pressured to presume that modernism is proper philosophy for an adult. But he embraces the strategy of returning to the childlike. "When fundamentals are doubted, as at present, we must try to recover the candor and wonder of the child; the unspoilt realism and objectivity of innocence."[80] He adds, "we must invoke

The Mother's Smile

the most wild and soaring sort of imagination; the imagination that can see what is there." As we'll see shortly, Chesterton commends returning to the philosophy of the nursery, a metaphysics of childhood.

Mother's smile gifts Baby with the philosophical structure of seeing and being seen in intimate encounter and ongoing communion. She sets the paradigm and the practice for our involvement with our world in knowing. As per this chapter, for her babe she is literally the face of reality itself. She opens a world to the tiny child—an "ontological paradise."

Yes—or No?—to Reality

Embedded in this encounter is the simplest matter of the human person's fundamental orientation to the real. Each of us lives out a deepest-level orientation to the world. We maintain an implicit posture, about which we exercise a tacit choice, a consent or rejection. Human persons body forth such a choice in contrast to, say, a dog or cat. A dog, it seems obvious, exercises no choice in the matter! A dog could never opt out of involvement the real.

Balthasar claims that "the soul's fundamental orientation to the world is affirmation and joy in being."[81] I take this to be saying that at our deepest level, each person ("the soul") orients to the world in which we find ourselves ("being"), and we do so in affirmation and joy. "Affirmation" is living a yes. This is the orientation we are meant to live out in our humanness. Human persons are meant for love of and communion with reality.

There lies at the heart of any person's involvement with the real a consent—else we are not involved, or it is not the real as it is most fully with which we are involved. The small child's orientation to reality is first of all a yes. Mother's smiling welcome forges us in affirmation of the real. We are shaped philosophically to consent to the real.

The key role of consent to the real is evident in knowing. In my philosophy of knowing, covenant epistemology, pledge lies at the heart of knowing. As a professor, I have always been convinced

Reality

that a student's consent to carry out the coursework I prescribed is critical to the venture. We love—and pledge—in order to know. Intimately related is our consent to the real.

The human person's primal orientation to the real is affirmation and it is joy, according to Balthasar. Robert Spaemann defines joy simply: joy is always an openness to reality. And, remarks Spaemann, "the openness to reality that is perfectly adequate is called love."[82] I believe that human persons are meant to be lovers of the real.

I can't think of better epitomizers of a stance of affirmation and joy in the real than very small children, can you? And what of our adult selves? Is it somehow superior if we have outgrown this childlike rapture? If so, this is a call to return to that natural astonishment. Chesterton writes: "This at least seems to me the main problem"—for his book, *Orthodoxy*, for philosophers, for us all—"how can we contrive to be at once astonished at the world and yet at home in it?"[83] We may so contrive this if we return to joyous affirmation, our fundamental orientation to the real.

But unlike dogs, human persons have a choice not to consent but rather to dissent from the real. Is yours or mine a posture of yes, or is it a posture of no? Affirmation or rejection? A posture of no, according to philosopher Josef Pieper, is what is meant by the sin of acedia. Acedia is "a refusal to consent to being" (that is, to the real).[84] When I first read this definition of acedia some years ago, in the margin I wrote: "—*Mea culpa!*" I sensed what I had not yet realized, that in some ways I myself was living a no, and that this was a matter to confess. I now see that my personal sense of nonexistence and my skeptical posture with regard to the real expressed this no, at the time without my realizing it. Consent or acedia, saying yes or saying no to the real: this is a philosophical matter.

A posture of yes to the real by no means baptizes blind, incautious yesses. For one thing, it is logically, not just physically, impossible to say yes to every single thing. To say yes to one thing is to count the cost of commitment with respect to many others. As a child grows up, it's either baseball or piano, for example. In prudent maturity, a no to some things just is part of a yes to the ones we

The Mother's Smile

consent to. An artist (and an author) simply has to say no at some point—or the work (or the self) is destroyed. True, we look to the wisdom of authoritative guides to guide our choices. But recognize that this also involves consent: to the right guides—to this guide and not that one. In contrast, acedia is saying no, on general principle, in a deep-seated way, to reality. Acedia rejects the real.

The modernist outlook is arguably intrinsically acedic: it is a philosophical refusal to consent to the real. People in modernity suspect reality—its existence or its generosity, its dignity. Or we high-handedly appropriate it for our own purposes. We teach critique, not consent, to our students, in the name of scholarship. Many people today get by, in life, by checking out, being absent, disengaged, bored. Modernity seems continually to spawn devices that draw us to opt for the virtual and to absent ourselves in indifference to the real. Being passionate about the real is deemed "not cool," not popular. We deem unsafe simple trust in reality. Although it may seem safe to shut out reality, this implicit posture of no brings with it the latent anxiety common in our modern age.

Thus it is that succumbing to the implicit disorientation of modernity expresses a philosophical acedia of which we may not even have been aware. On the other hand, returning with intentionality to a natural metaphysics of childhood dispels that disorientation and reinstates affirmation and joy in the real. As per Chesterton: philosophy is astonished belonging, at home with the ever-opening real.

Is Reality There?

Now let's consider this related matter: Is there a reality beyond me, independently of my knowing it? This is the philosophical question of realism. Much philosophical study has been devoted to this—including my own. This was my urgent adolescent question. I chose this topic for my PhD dissertation. I presumed that I was a solitary, disembodied mind, certain only of my mental contents, with no proof for the world beyond my perception and conception of it. Markedly, I displayed the influence of Descartes' modern

Reality

vision. I was, philosophically, an anti-realist. But Baby is a philosophical realist—as was I at my own birth.

In my dissertation I reflected on many philosophical positions on this matter. Among them is Hilary Putnam's "internal realism." This then-popular proposal confines "reality" to the objects of my mind (in ongoing deference to Descartes' picture). Now I find that philosopher Robert Spaemann directly challenges internal realism. He reports that he even raised this matter in person with Putnam himself. Spaemann posed to Putnam "the case in which we ourselves are the object of others' speech—when we are in fact the others of others."[85] Someone speaks about us, perhaps to a third person, perhaps to us. We are not tempted to believe that their speech of us is all there is to us, are we? Especially if we feel they are mistaken! In the experience he describes, "we are unable seriously to believe that our existence reduces to another's perception of me." Spaemann reports that Putnam, however, dismissed this case as an exception rather than a critical and fundamental experience.

Spaemann vehemently disagrees that this case is an exception. Being the others of others is no exception, but rather the *paradigm* for our relationship to reality and for knowledge in general. "The mode of givenness of other persons is the paradigm for the givenness of reality in general."[86] Reality is an on-its-ownness beyond what it discloses to us in any given encounter. "The really real is that which something is in itself and for itself, and thus beyond its being an object for others."[87]

"In relation to other persons," writes Spaemann, "we can't avoid being metaphysical realists—especially when we realize that we ourselves are the others of others."[88] Metaphysical realism, in dissent from "internal realism" (the term itself harbors a contradiction), holds that reality does exist independently of my knowing it. But metaphysical realism requires that there are others, says Spaemann. "Does the sphere of reality extend beyond the sphere of my consciousness? Only if there are others—other beings for whom it is true that I have consciousness. If there weren't, the two would be identical; and there would be no reason to reflect on it!"[89]

The Mother's Smile

Is metaphysical realism the natural presumption of the baby, formed in the mother's welcoming smile? Yes. Realism is forged in the mother's smile. Mother sees me, welcomes me, speaks of me; I am here! But I myself do not reduce to her perception of me. I am real—my subjectivity is objective. I myself am the other of Mother. In humble fact, Mother was here first—here even before I was a twinkle in my father's eye.

Real Things as Personlike Others

But then the child works this connection in the other direction as well: as with Mother, real things are there, beyond and before, irreducible to my involvement with them. Spaemann adjures us to attribute something like selfhood to other entities.[90] Moving beyond the matter of *whether*, we turn to *what*: to the "otherly" nature of reality itself. For Baby, in Baby's natural metaphysics of childhood, Mother has set the pattern for the real. The real is personed or personlike, like Mother.

The essay of Spaemann's from which I have been drawing is titled, "In Defense of Anthropomorphism." To view things anthropomorphically means to consider them persons or personlike, like ourselves. If we are saying that Mother has set the pattern for the real, in effect we are being anthropomorphic. Is anthropomorphism what we have been born into? Is it responsible to accredit and sustain anthropomorphism in our involvement with the real?

Spaemann writes that anthropomorphism is generally considered a deficient way of thinking. But, he asks, "is this a childish relic?"[91] Is it a primitive way of thinking? "Ancient thought always viewed the inanimate world anthropomorphically." Is anthropomorphism something we should reject, or return to?

Spaemann notes that this is a common modernist criticism. For knowledge to be "objective," modernity presumes, the knower must be uninvolved: we must resist importing our personal bias into what we perceive. But "my response to this objection is that we have to view a thing anthropomorphically if we want to do justice to it," he writes. "We can only speak adequately of it on the

Reality

basis of the conscious life that we ourselves are." Anthropomorphism indeed seems childish and primitive "if we have resolved to view inanimate matter as unreal, and thus as exhausting its reality in being ready to hand for living beings or, on the other hand, in being nothing but objects for science." But, he says, "if we attribute reality to material being in the sense that has been developed here, by contrast, then we think of it as coexisting with us."[92] In view of our conversation here about a metaphysics of childhood, our natural way of seeing the world, childlike anthropomorphism would be something to which we should return.

Spaemann shows that much of our best understanding of the world requires us thinking anthropomorphically in order to make sense of it: causality, movement, potentiality, freedom, anticipation, goals, striving. He cites one contrasting example. Infinitesimal calculus does not provide an understanding of movement. "We can calculate it only at the price of eliminating the phenomenon of movement as such."[93]

According to Spaemann, for the philosophical modernist, the world is not anthropomorphic; instead, it is actually anthropocentric. To treat the world anthropomorphically is truthful. To treat the world anthropocentrically is manipulative. Modernity "does not ask what truly is and what therefore has the character of existing side-by-side with us, but asks instead how it appears to us as object and how it is able to be manipulated by us." In anthropomorphism, things are like us. In anthropocentrism, things are merely for us. Objects merely for us stand over against us and we have nothing in common with them. "To want to understand reality as it is in itself means to view it under the aspect of some degree of similarity with us."[94]

Anthropomorphism is to view something as *like us*, not merely *for us*. Mothers view us, and we view them, as other, like oneself, not for one's own use. As Spaemann notes, Mother and I *recognize* each other. "For even with regard to the inanimate material world that is distant from us, we have to say that to regard it as real, to recognize it as something that exists in some sense in itself, means to view it under the aspect of similarity with us, and thus anthropomorphically, not as an object, but as something that shares in reality with us."[95] To view things anthropomorphically postures us in due regard for the other; it postures us to love and seek communion with the real.

Even a thing, as a thing, is an anthropomorphism. "Bodies are things that retain a unity with themselves over a certain period of time," Spaemann writes.[96] "For there to be understanding or a designation as real, there must be recognition of similarity to ourselves."[97] Real being is "being with" or it just isn't real. To reject anthropomorphism is to reject things. Modernity rejects both. To reject things, Spaemann infers, is also to reject ourselves. In modernity, "Man is the last to dissolve, but when he does, even the anthropocentrism that is science fades away."[98]

Thus it is that Baby's formative encounter with Mother issues in a metaphysics of childhood which says yes joyously to a reality patterned after Mother as personlike. And Baby extends this courteous, generous presumption to real things. For Baby, there is Mother, there is Me, and there are other things nearby in my world.

The real is . . . things: coherent, irreducible things in some way looking to welcome me. Mother is my first real thing. I am formed in mutual response with her. In turn, I respond to other near things in kind, as that "entire paradise of reality" opens before me.

A Metaphysics of Childhood

What follows is a time-honored philosophical account of reality simple enough for me to christen it a natural "metaphysics of childhood." In *Doorway to Artistry*, it is stunning enough for me to speak of things as "everyday jewels of the real."[99] And it is a vision of the real that we receive firsthand in the rapturous gaze of Mother.

Here I express it briefly—as do its medieval originators. But I acknowledge that it takes time to soak in it and come round to it— especially given our uphill battle against the modernist antirealist outlook we inherit. I believe that starting to think this way restores us to a childlike, exuberant splashing in the real. To convey my

Reality

beginning sense of it: reality is aptly represented as a perennial Christmas morning showering of love overflowing in gifts.

The first thing about things is that they exist.[100] Our first response may be—"So?" That ho-hum response wrongheadedly overlooks the astonishing might-not-being at the heart of things. Things might not be, but they are. This is just what we said about our own existence in an earlier chapter. A thing is: a thing "izzes," as one philosopher playfully and helpfully expresses it.[101] A thing is an izzing arrival, something more like a giant fountain thrusting upward. A thing is more an event than an object. A thing announces: "Here I am!" Existence is no mere check in the box. Astonishment is continually apropos, as is gratitude for these gifts. The Holy Scriptures identify this lively izzing as God's act of creation, here, now, here, now.

This izzing continues on to permeate its things. Things characteristically overflow in activity and possibility. The real, says Schindler, "is by nature more than itself," given to lively, surprising excess.[102] Rowan Williams writes that "things are more than they are."[103] Williams, writing about artistry, sees artistry as tapping into and actualizing this more. So does any study or serious pursuit. From the beginning of my attention to Polanyi, I was enthralled by this premier discoverer's confident claim: we know we have made contact with reality by our unspecifiable sense of indeterminate but inexhaustive future manifestations.[104] This is a signature feature of reality itself.

There are a handful of features of this izzing arrival that permeate all existing things just by virtue of their existence, which transcend the thing's specific essential defining characteristics. They have been known for centuries as "transcendentals."

Here is the traditional list: Thing. One. Something. Beautiful. Good. True. Existence brims with irreducibly coherent unities (thing, one) relating to other things (and especially to human persons) (something) to self-show (beauty), self-give (goodness), and self-say (truth).[105] It's a tiny thing, but aptly allusive: I've playfully called these, "facets" of things, the everyday jewels of the real.[106] The word contains "face." The facets present. To deny them would be defacing.

The Mother's Smile

This account of the real could only exist where love is the fundamental medium of all there is. Love could only be the fundamental medium of all there is if things have been set free to exist in their lively ownness. What is distinctive about the Christian doctrine of creation is that God as God is active, perfect love itself. So God's creating, in every atom and second, is a perfect giving away to things to stand own their own. A thing receives its ownness as a gift from beyond. Honoring things always bears witness to God. However, it is essential to the Christian doctrine of creation that things stand in their ownness.

Philosopher Michael Hanby writes that a philosophical account of things in their thisness and particularity "is distinctively at home in the Christian doctrine of creation."[107] The Greeks fell short of accounting for things in their particularity, he says, since they lacked an account of God as radically transcendent. Modern reductivism, as we will note presently, according to Hanby, explicitly rejects things in their particularity.

In the rapturous welcoming gaze of the smiling mother, the newborn beholds a gift, a real thing in the world: Mother. Mother is one thing, astonishing, brimming existence and love, already an active, ongoing, presencing, addressing me, relating me to others, freely self-showing, self-giving, and self-saying. Things give themselves generously, in noble courtesy. Baby responds in astonished delight to real things. And he relates to them in courteous reciprocation, by following Mother's lead. Mother sets the paradigm for all other things.

In his book *Orthodoxy*, G. K. Chesterton seconds the child's reliable natural love of existing things. He argues that the fairy tales he learned as a small child at the knee of his nurse afforded him a truer grasp of reality than modernism was pressing him, as an adult, to embrace. "My first and last philosophy, that which I believe in with unbroken certainty, I learnt in the nursery."[108] Fairy tales founded in him the conviction that "this world is a wild and startling place, which might have been quite different, but which is quite delightful."

Reality

For Chesterton, fairy book terms—charm, spell, enchantment—aptly "express the arbitrariness of the fact and its mystery." He represents his strongest emotion: "that life was as precious as it was puzzling." Indeed, "Can I thank no one for the birthday present of birth?"[109] Existence is a surprise, but it is a pleasant surprise, he writes.

But Chesterton avers that

> this elementary wonder, however, is not a mere fancy derived from the fairy tales; on the contrary, all the fire of the fairy tales is derived from this . . . . [W]e all like astonishing tales because they touch the nerve of the ancient instinct of astonishment. This is proved by the fact that when we are very young children we do not need fairy tales: we only need tales. Mere life is interesting enough. . . . This proves that even nursery tales only echo an almost pre-natal leap of interest and amazement.[110]

Chesterton's whimsical wisdom converges with a metaphysic forged in the mother's rapturous welcome, a welcoming real that is already elvish, an astonishing homeland.

Robert Farrar Capon also affirms the primacy of things. In his *Supper of the Lamb* he offers his defense for being an amateur cook—amateur, meaning lover. "Man's real work is to look at the things of the world and to love them for what they are. That is, after all, what God does, and man was not made in God's image for nothing. The fruits of his attention can be seen in all the arts, crafts, and sciences."[111] Capon is famous for proposing an hour-long encounter with an onion! "You will note, to begin with, that the onion is a thing, a being, just as you are. Savor that for a moment. The two of you sit here in mutual confrontation."[112] He speaks of the onion as "this gorgeous paradigm of unnecessary being"!

Returning to the philosophical paradigm of the mother's smiling welcome and to our natural metaphysics of childhood restores us to an orientation of yes to the world. It restores the other as personlike, welcoming, brimming with loved mystery. It restores the irreducibility of things, the everyday jewels of the real.

The Mother's Smile

It reinstates our love of the real. It restores our philosophical birthright, and honors our natal philosophical formation.

Restoring Our Childhood Vision of the Real

In pointed contrast, the agenda of modernity has been to de-face the real. Modernity exalts, not things, but their utility. If intrinsic interest is eclipsed by instrumental interest, writes Schindler, "the very quality of our attention cannot help but be transformed [that is, altered for the worse]; we will want to know them just to the point that they reveal how they can serve that ulterior purpose. This implies that our attention to them is directed immediately to something else."[113]

Modernity is characterized by a loss of intrinsic interest in things. Modernity embraced the very opposite of the primacy of things; it embraced reductivism. Reductivism poses that everything reduces to its tiniest components with no remainder. It poses that "the thing" is an unnecessary, even "occult," add-on.

Schindler replies almost defiantly: "We answer: what is 'added' is the presence of the whole as such, which may not seem to matter if we are interested only in the useful information that can be extracted, but it matters a great deal if we wish to retain an understanding of knowledge as intimate contact with reality. It matters if reality matters."[114]

The "presence of the whole as such," irreducibly coherent as it is, is a kind of face. It brims with beauty. It gives itself in love, while simultaneously remaining other in freedom. It is filled with lively meaning, simultaneously readable and mysterious. "Here I am!" "Welcome!" It invites us to mutuality, intimacy, and communion. Along with rejecting the primacy of irreducible things, in its reductivism modernity desecrates the face.

With a little thought we can see that reductivism is inherently contradictory: we can make no sense of any components in the absence of the thing. The parts wouldn't be parts without presuming the whole. So modernity's "reality" is founded on a contradiction. But thankfully, given what we have embraced in the gaze of our mothers, we persist through our lives to presume implicitly the primacy of things, even in our attempts to deny them.

For us to see how the mother's smile philosophically forms our philosophy of reality, we must also have restored—or let it restore—our philosophy of reality! Having done so, as with knowing, we find we have a match: what better means to such a vision of the real than in our early beholding of the delighted face of Mother!

The lively, welcoming, responsive, pregnant real seeks and needs noticing delight and regard from us human persons who are capable of consenting in affirmation and joy to it. "What the cosmos seeks," writes German philosopher Ferdinand Ulrich, "is an ever deeper Yes to be spoken to it, an affirmation of its being."[115] He commends "thinking as thanking."[116] "The fundamental act of human existence is gratitude, he writes." In gratefully receiving our own existence, we "set free all things in their being," reciprocally inviting the real.

As Capon pronounces: "The world needs all the lovers—amateurs—it can get. It is a gorgeous old place, full of clownish graces and beautiful drolleries, and it has enough textures, tastes, and smell to keep us intrigued for more time than we have. Unfortunately, however, our response to its loveliness is not always delight; it is, far more often than it should be, boredom. And that is not only odd, it is tragic; for boredom is not neutral—it is the fertilizing principle of unloveliness. . . . There, then, is the role of the amateur: to look the world back to grace."[117]

We desperately need to rehabilitate our vision of the real as ever lively, pregnant with more, and reaching out to welcome us. In the rapturous gaze of Mother, and Baby's response in kind, Baby is formed philosophically in affirmation and joy in reality. Baby readily takes up the practice of looking the world back to grace, carrying it out in exemplary fashion (as Grandmamà knows well!). Baby takes to the love of things. According to Schindler: philosophy just is "an all-encompassing love of the real, a love that is only deepened by the Christian faith."[118] The rapturous, welcoming smile of Mother, and the noticing regard of others, forms us philosophically for our purpose: a life of lively communion with the real.

7

The Other

Although we have repeatedly spoken of "the other," this matter deserves its own chapter. The rapturous, welcoming gaze of our mothers and the noticing regard of certain family and friends form us philosophically to recognize, address, and enact due regard to the other. If Mother is my first other, if my existence requires the other, if the real is the other, and if my knowing encounters and responds to the other—if, in other words, my whole reason for existence is communion with the other, then the other is philosophically crucial.

Other refers to another being—the world, a person, or thing—beyond me. Although people sometimes take the use of "other" to be dismissive, objectifying, and phobic, I have in mind the exact opposite. The other is there, the same as me and different from me, due my regard by virtue of their existing. For the other, I too am other. So my treatment of the other rebounds on me.

The Other

Mother and Me: Union and Abiding Otherness

"Mother" contains "other." She is our first other, and she sets the bar on behalf of all others. Mother comes from beyond (and before) in welcome. Baby beholds Mother. Baby beholds Mother beholding Baby. All this takes the form, not of skepticism, inference, and proof, but of recognition, address, and invitation: "So! It is You!"

Mother, as I, the infant, bask in her gaze and respond in kind, forms me in due regard for the other. In the philosophically formative gaze of the loving mother the tiny child has come to their own existence and irreducible personhood as the other of Mother. In turn the child apprehends the reality and dignity of the other beyond our knowing as essential to knowing and the real. The known, the real, the world beyond me is—ought to be—other, with respect to the knower—with respect to me. Remember Capon: "You will note, to begin with, that the onion is a thing, a being, just as you are. Savor that for a moment. The two of you sit here in mutual confrontation."

Here is a key quotation that shapes this little book. In reflecting on Hans Urs von Balthasar's anchoring motif of the mother's smile, D. C. Schindler contrasts Balthasar's approach to that of other contemporary philosophical responses to modernism: "Balthasar's deeper aim is to preserve an abiding otherness in the completed act of knowledge even within the soul's union

In the philosophically formative gaze of the loving mother the tiny child has come to their own existence and irreducible personhood as the other of Mother. In turn the child apprehends the reality and dignity of the other beyond our knowing as essential to knowing and the real.

with its object."[119] Some contemporary philosophies continue to concede modernism: they stay within the knower's experience, attending to an internal object, as we noted before. This paradigm of knowing remains egological and possessive, as Schindler and Balthasar have written, thus fundamentally a disregard of the reality and value of the other. But the true end of knowing is communion with an other in its abiding otherness, beyond me, but also inviting my best efforts to know it.

Schindler defines "the completed act of knowledge" as the knower's union with its object. Knowing is intimate encounter, in which knower and known come to union and identity. But it is a union that preserves the "abiding otherness" of the known. "Abiding" otherness implies that the personlike own-ness of the other continues in this "generous opposition of freedom." Mother gives herself; she does not (and should not) give herself away. Mother and child together instantiate a union that preserves otherness; together they forge the shaping philosophical paradigm of Baby's future involvement with the real.

Union and abiding otherness, though contrasting and complementary, unfold together. The only way this could be is if our knowing is a bonding of healthy, mutual love. Love non-possessively preserves the abiding otherness of the other. It is a bond that actually enhances the abiding otherness of the other. Where there is true otherness, there is love; where there is love, there is true otherness, flourishing in that mutuality.

As I noted before, Robert Spaemann writes that the joy-filled openness to reality that is perfectly adequate is called love. He defines love as the other's becoming real for me. The other ceases to revolve around me, to be an object for me. Mother and we ourselves are, and we learn to see ourselves as part of the other's world, just as they are part of our world. Love, the other, and the real come together philosophically to epitomize our richest involvement with the world.

The Other

Modernity's "Object"

Our modernist outlook was forged with the two-sided agenda to exalt the self and to devalue the world for purposes other than the other for itself. Where the self is rendered the absolute arbiter of knowledge, all the world beyond the knower becomes an object legitimated only in reference to the knower and the knower's use of it. It is an object no longer beyond the knower. Things are no longer things; they reduce to objects for this subject. And subject and object fall into unstable opposition, endlessly vying each with the other for the upper hand.

This move suits modernity admirably. It issues carte blanche to the self's aggressive mission of pragmatic mastery and control over nature. No "other" remains beyond the self to exert a personed claim on the self's involvement with the world beyond. No "other" remains beyond the self even to invite the self to be a self. No "other" remains to be delighted in for its own sake. Schindler remarks that in modernity knowledge appropriates "only by eliminating the 'otherness' of its object."[120]

For modernism, objects possess no intrinsic meaning, but only the meaning their masters attribute to them. As such they are eminently manipulable for pragmatic ends and human mastery. Knowledge, as modernity understands it, is domination and commodification, apropos because of objectification. All we know, and need to know, is how to put the objects in view to work. What we moderns typically take to be knowledge is far from the intimate encounter of intelligible communion of others one with another. This penchant of modernity also accounts for the more common, negative connotation of "other": the other is something that we have belittled, and that we deem an antagonizing threat.

As we have marked before, Spaemann claims that modernity denatured nature through the despotic objectification of nature. Our best fundamental challenge to the modern age must involve attributing something like selfhood to other entities. We need to restore a fundamental regard for the other. This is to accord primacy to the other in reality.

The Mother's Smile

Existence, Knowing, and Reality: Each for the Other

The other is essential philosophically. For us to have even the most fundamental sense of our own existence, it takes an other, for whom we see that we are other. It takes an other in whose gaze we see ourselves being seen.

Philosophical modernism's telltale rejection of the other is just what leads it to abandon metaphysics. But the primacy of the other in knowing points to the "abiding other" that is real, as we saw in the last chapter. In knowing as it should be, knower and known enact an interpersoned, mutually transformative, intimate encounter and unfolding communion. Encounter and communion require two centers of presence, each other to the other, and for the other: involved together in mutuality. Reality, then, is personlike, with a dignity worthy of our regard. As we have seen, Spaemann writes "in defense of anthropomorphism."

Where reality is other, knowing requires the other. As we have seen, John Macmurray writes categorically:

> The first knowledge, then, is knowledge of the personal Other—the Other with whom I am in communication, who responds to my cry and cares for me. This is the starting point of all knowledge and is presupposed at every stage of its subsequent development. . . . The knowledge of the Other is the absolute presupposition of all knowledge, and as such is necessarily indemonstrable.[121]

Also:

> This original reference to the Other is of a definitive importance. It is the germ of rationality. For the character that distinguishes rational from non-rational experience, in all the expressions of reason, is its reference to the Other-than-myself.[122]

When we considered knowing, we said that it is at first *receptive*. Thinking is being moved by an other, according to Schindler. At the same time, it is *active*. It is by definition ecstatic—reaching beyond itself to be out there in and with the other from the beginning.

The Other

Best practices in knowing are those that invite the real, those that are best suited to knowing a personal other. Love, pledge, noticing regard, attentive listening, fidelity, obedience, communion itself: these form a kind of "epistemological etiquette," a noble courtesy toward the yet to be known. These are effective; but the point is that they themselves confer due dignity upon the other. If you want to know the thing as it really is, you must honor the thing as it really is, delighting in knowing it entirely for its own sake.

Knowing fundamentally requires regard for the other. Knowing is communion with the real; human persons were made for communion with the real. Communion is mutual interpersoned involvement and understanding. (It is also festive!)[123] The mother smiling at her child is not merely an example of this, or merely a helpful analogy. Rather, mother and child, face to face, is philosophically paradigmatic, and that *en face* is philosophically, fundamentally formative of our involvement with the world.

How you characterize knowing and how you characterize reality connect integrally. Modernity's implicit philosophy has reduced reality to our knowing it, and our knowing it—conceived of as amassing information to the end of human mastery—to disavowal and disregard of the other. When we return to embrace the mother's welcome as philosophically formative and paradigmatic, we restore both reality and knowing because we reinstate regard for the other.

Regard for the Other

Robin Wall Kimmerer, a Native American and a botanist, has contributed an award-winning book of essays, *Braiding Sweetgrass*.[124] In it she describes a traditional indigenous approach to the living earth, contrasting it with the modern scientific approach as it is conventionally understood. Kimmerer helps us imagine and emulate what regard for the other looks like. I invite you to experience her inspiring book on your own, for I find in her insights far more convergence with my proposals than I can share here. Plus, *Sweetgrass* should be indwelt, in due regard for the other, so as to understand and see.

The Mother's Smile

Out of far greater personal suffering and sensitivity than mine, Kimmerer charges the Western modernist culture with ravaging a land in which we may belong only as we offer due regard to other, nonhuman, or more-than-human, beings. Righting our relationship with the land indicates the need for a massive reworking of Western presumptions about private property and wealth; for Kimmerer's native approach begins with the assertion that no one owns the land. Sovereign beings, human or non human others, are not to be owned and thus depersonalized.

Her remarks suggest that her problem with modernity is fundamentally philosophical. The problem is not science but "the scientific worldview": "a cultural context that uses science and technology to reinforce reductionist, materialist economics and political agendas."[125] It perpetuates the illusion of dominance and control, and the separation of knowledge from responsibility.

Modernity, she says, reduces subjects to objects. She concurs that modernity abhors anthropomorphism as a threat to objectivity. Instead, "we must say of the universe that it is a communion of subjects, not a collection of objects."[126]

An indigenous approach regards our surrounding world as lively, non-human (even more-than-human) beings. Plants and other beings are the ones who care for us, give us all we need, and teach us how to be human. They welcome us, respond to us, love us back. Kimmerer repeatedly commends recognizing their abundant gifts, enacting gratitude (especially in greetings and ceremonies), embracing the ongoing relationship and reciprocity that gifts (in contrast to commodities) always entail, pledging allegiance in a "Bill of Responsibilities," covenanting to the rules for an Honorable Harvest.[127] She commends ceremony as a vehicle of belonging, of saying, "Here we are." To which the land responds: "Ohh, *here* are the people who know how to say thank you!"[128] The land knows you, she writes, even when you are lost.

Flourishing requires reciprocity, because all flourishing is mutual. We need these other beings; and they need us. Sweetgrass, for example, grows only in the places where it is respectfully and gently harvested. This vision accords with philosopher Ferdinand

The Other

Ulrich's memorable pronouncement: "What the cosmos seeks is an ever deeper Yes to be spoken to it, an affirmation of its being."

A native approach honors non-human beings as other. Kimmerer reveals that indigenous languages are 70 percent verbs, in contrast to 30 percent in the English language. One would never assign a noun to something unless it is dead. Anything alive requires a verb. In addition to plants, things include, for example, ground and rivers and places. My favorite is that *bay* is a verb: "to be a bay"! I note the kinship here with the act of existence, which we have seen that modernity effaces. I mark that Kimmerer says that toddlers understand animacy! Kimmerer commends a "grammar of animacy"—"so that we might be truly at home."[129]

Ever so sadly, from Kimmerer's perspective, many modern colonizers act as if we are homeless, as if we are not native, as if we do not have both feet off the boat and on the shore.[130] We do not belong to our world. In revoking the other, we have lost ourselves and our being at home. But—"we all were once indigenous," writes Kimmerer; so we may yet reclaim our membership in the cultures of gratitude that formed our old relationships with the living earth.

We were all indigenous once—and we were all born into our mother's welcome. In this little book of mine, I am advocating for a natural, childlike philosophy, which can return us to being at home in the world, and to which we may return. In returning to our natal philosophy, we return to being at home; we return to animacy.

Our philosophical formation in a natural metaphysics of childhood, to be what it is, requires the other. Our selfhood, our existence, our knowing, and reality all require the other. Our involvement in encounter requires mutuality. Our own flourishing and the flourishing of the others that make up our world depends profoundly on our philosophical healing. The world needs our yes, our due regard for it as other. An amateur cook must regard an onion as other, according to Capon. The arts and sciences are meant to behold the world as other and look it back to grace. For there to be love, there must be an other. To be the lovers of the real we were designed to be, we require this outlook and ministration.

8

Friends

So it is that all of us human persons begin to be formed philosophically in the rapturous, welcoming gaze of our mother. Arriving into the arms of our mother at birth and receiving her steady, delighted regard forms our sense of our own existence, our sense of the lively real, and our encounter and communion with it in our best knowing and all our involvements.

Now it is time to make good on the promise that all this also pertains to the faces of certain others in our lives, a few "operative" ones. The childhood philosophy nascently forming in the mother's smile is sustained and forwarded in the faces of friends, over the years. Friends serve distinctively in our maturation. And that includes a kind of retroactive consolidating, a maturing, of the welcoming face of the other. It also includes a kind of consolidating hope, looking forward.

Not all of our friends will be this kind of friend! And we need this kind of friend. We need a few friends who see us, in whose gaze we see ourselves being seen, whose faces display noticing regard for us. In these faces we find further philosophical formation.

Friends

Dad is an all-important early face, a second mother, a second friend—and if tragedy strikes, he is first of each. I am told that someone asked award-winning author Toni Morrison to which course of study she owed her literary prowess. She replied, "Oh—no course of study! I owe it to the fact that when I was a child, whenever I walked into the room where my father was, his face lit up." And Elizabeth Moltmann-Wendel, in *I Am My Body* writes of how boys but especially girls need to see a "glint" in their father's eyes, a glint of admiration for their body and soul as beautiful and desirable. If this is lacking for little girls, "from then on too much emptiness and a longing for fullness dog girls' lives, and that can become the drama of their lives. . . . Where a 'glint' is provoked, security grows. Where insecurity prevails, women allow judgments to be foisted on them which are not their own."[131]

Here are the sorts of people who might be your particular friend or friends: in addition to Mom and Dad, siblings and grandparents, in unfolding relationships as we grow up. Spouses. Teachers and coaches. Pastors. Neighbors and colleagues. Children and grandchildren! Students. It can be groups of people, not just individuals: support groups, football teams, jazz ensembles. And I want to include not just persons but the other nouns: places and things we are blessed to discover and come to know in intimate communion. Places: neighborhoods, basketball courts, alma maters. Things: an old climbing rose, the clay thrown on our wheel growing into a pot, an animal we rescue, a quadratic equation we figure out, a book and its world.

Why must there be friends who see us and in whose gaze we see ourselves? Here are some reasons for needing them. We don't remember our earliest time with Mother. Plus, things happen to Mother—normal things and abnormal things. If we have suffered from the inattention or loss of dear faces earlier in our lives, certain friends can be the special instruments of our healing.

Also, as may well have been in my case, from childhood, or in adolescence, we may block that precious gaze. As you'll see, I've only returned to it in these later years of my life.

The Mother's Smile

Then, obviously, we grow up. The friendship of two more mature persons has a correspondingly maturing influence. Plus, friends share our particular visions, loves, and enterprises. Friends add distinctively pertinent perspectives to our own. They can occupy an especially significant position from which to see us and show us ourselves. But these friends are linked in solidarity with us. They are committedly for us.

As for the discoveries we make, our involvements with nonhuman real things: we "need" these friends because this is just our privileged purpose: communion with the real. This just is the corollary of the philosophy into which we have been born. And as we'll also say again here, real things need us to see them with delighted regard. We need operative faces; things need our operative faces. Our knowing involvement with the things of our lives needs to be a seeing and being seen.

There must be mothers, and there must be others. Others must carry on the philosophical ministration our mothers began. As it was with Mother, it's as my friend or friends see me that I sense I am here, worthy of regard. I can live a posture of yes toward the world. They enact with me the very model of great knowing: friendship with the real. They hold forth the very model of my purpose in life: communion with the real. We practice regularly with our friends the noble courtesy due to all the things of the world. In our friendship with them we instantiate the love that is the fabric of this universe. They can be to us earthly glimpses of the face of God.

> There must be mothers, and there must be others. Others must carry on the philosophical ministration our mothers began.

Friends are key to our becoming more and more ourselves, actualizing our possibilities. We grow into their confident vision. Philosopher Caroline Simon has defined love in this way: love is "imagining the other's

Friends

destiny truly."[132] This powerful phrase expresses it so well. As a real thing yourself, you are brimming with possibilities. You are more than you are, as Rowan Williams and others have said. You are more than you yourself can see that you are. A friend who sees you sees both you and your more. They imagine your destiny truly—as opposed to "fiction making"! (Simon's apt term.) They see you and know you well, perhaps better than you know yourself. It can be that we entrust ourselves to their vision of us, even overruling our own limited or mistaken self-perception, that we grow more fully into ourselves. We mature.

And friends are key to our seeing the greater possibilities of the real. This is especially the ministration of a teacher or any authoritative guide—especially those who see how we ourselves are distinctively related to reality's possibilities.

Here are stories of a couple people who saw me, and in whose gaze I have seen myself. I share them to model those you find in your own life in response to these questions: Who noticed you? Who notices you? Whose are the philosophically operative faces in your life?

My Sister, Judy

There was another in my family who saw me formatively. That was my sister, Judy. Aged twelve when I was born, she told me that my birth was wonder itself: it was as if she was being given a living doll! I was special to her from the beginning. One old family movie of her sixteenth birthday shows her, surrounded by friends, drawing and lifting a bibbed little me into her lap so that I could help her blow out her candles.

Judy was always going away and returning. She was a masterful pianist in demand even from my birth. She left for college when I started first grade. I was nine when she married. I was always counting the days till she would return, crossing them off on my calendar. I knew that she wanted to get back to me. I was confident that she would see me when she came!

The Mother's Smile

Although she was always leaving, Judy continually schemed to get me to where she was so I could be with her. She even worked it out for me to spend a week with her at college! She took me along when she had organs to play, and even had me join her on the bench to push or pull stops for her. She had our mother drive me halfway to where she lived as a newlywed for a rendezvous and visit. One time she arranged for me to ride a steam train excursion with her train-fan brother-in-law to bring me to the place where she was living. She merrily insisted that a youthful me, terrified though I was, ride the city buses to rendezvous points downtown for shopping and visiting.

Over the years when I lived far away, she always saved her weekly "allowance" to buy herself plane tickets to visit me. When I visited her, I was always a special guest, one who belonged at her side, whom she introduced with a flourish of delight to all others. Although she never made me feel badly if I opted not to come see her, I always knew I was wanted and welcome wherever she was. Even after her death, her entire family continues to welcome me as an honored, foregone conclusion.

I will forever treasure her words to me over the phone on the eve of the surgery that within a few months led to her death. "Remember," Judy chirped playfully, "I have always loved you!" True! Even as I write this, on my desk where I can see it is a photo of Judy, seated at a grand piano bedecked with Christmas lights and poinsettia, smiling back over her shoulder—at me. Yes, the faces of people who have passed away may have so registered within us that they remain operative. She continues to delight, and to cheer me on. I continue to see myself in her gaze of noticing regard.

When I was discovering that matter of not being noticed, I told Judy of this. Tears sprang into her eyes as she said, "Oh honey, I'm so sorry!" (which I quickly rejected as inapplicable in her case!). Then I asked her who had noticed her. It was the first time it had ever occurred to me to formulate this odd question. She promptly responded knowingly: "Oh! Granny Harvey noticed me!" Unbeknownst to Judy the child, it was Granny who, out of a meager widow's income, paid for Judy's piano lessons when our parents could not afford it. Judy and Granny roomed together, at home and also for several summers at a Christian conference at the ocean shore, where Judy played the piano and Granny ran the bookstore. When I was a small child, it was these two, Judy and Granny, whom I longed to see. (This is partly why I love the ocean; those conference grounds remain heaven on earth to me.) After Granny's decease, Judy always wore Granny's lovely opal ring. Though I am indebted to and grateful for the upbringing of my parents, Granny and Judy channeled a kind of special singling out, noticing love to me—one I feel sure was divine in origin.

My Colleague, Bob

Let me tell you about my philosophy colleague and dear friend, Bob Frazier. Dr. Robert M. Frazier has been the one and only official full-time philosophy colleague I have had in my professional work. Together we have been the philosophy program at Geneva College.

If you have read my other books or heard me speak, you have heard of Bob. From the beginning of Geneva College's consideration of me for a faculty position in the philosophy program alongside him, Bob already knew my scholarly work and pointedly welcomed me to join him. Driving me back to the airport after my interview, he said, "If you come, we will be friends." It was a pronouncement, not a prediction. For both of us, friendship (and mirth therein) became the signature of the philosophical life we shared with our colleagues and students.

Bob has deeply grasped, affirmed, abetted, and inspired my work and mission. He generously offered wise counsel and creative strategy, supplying the steady impetus for my professional output over these last couple decades. With his confident and creative, "What you want to do is this—," he would suggest the next steps I should take, the next books and papers I should write. He just presumed that I could do whatever it was. Bob was always my first reader; and I always felt that if he liked it (and he always did), it didn't matter what anyone else thought.

The Mother's Smile

Bob's solidarity with me was rock solid; his advocacy was unwavering. He listened to me and took me utterly seriously. It's in his noticing regard that I finally did come to sense the gravitas of my personhood.

Of course our friendship continues, although my retiring from the classroom has suspended its lively day-to-day expression—and Bob was the first to urge this move on to a life of writing, even at cost to himself and his own workload. A photo of the two of us at a December commencement, side by side and grinning, stands on my shelf where I see it from my desk. I have been enduringly formed in his noticing regard.

But I want to tell you about Bob's face! I don't mean any particular expression, but rather the frank, unqualified regard and particular delight that it always registered as he looked at me. I saw him seeing me. Over the years I grew to see myself as Bob sees me; I chose this visage, holding to his seeing me as more objective than my own subjective view. As a person, and also professionally, I have come to be who I am in his unwavering regard.

When I was teaching students at Geneva about this matter of the regard-filled face of certain others, I would give them my own example of Dr. Frazier. Many of them would begin to grin broadly, for they understood firsthand: they were recipients of his delighted notice also—especially the athletes, female and male! "The Fraze" is simply excellent at delighted noticing regard.

The Operative Faces in Your Life

Whose are the operative faces in your life? Who sees you? Who notices you with regard? Whose are the authoritative faces, in whose gaze of regard you see yourself being seen into your best self? As an exercise in class, I would have the students carry out what I now invite you to try. Grab a sheet of paper and a pencil. Using stick figures, sketch and label the people who see you. Put yourself in the center, and array the others around you, using relative size and proximity to your own stick figure to indicate importance or presence. Your parents will likely be there. Grandparents and other

Friends

family members can be key. You should sketch a spouse and a close friend or two. There might be a string of twelve or so schoolteachers, and a janitor or coach or youth pastor. There can be a band of brothers, a team, an ensemble, who sees you. Or your large Italian family who gather Sunday by Sunday.

In this stick figure reflection, we are showing graphically the friends whose gazes carry forward and sustain our philosophical formation. We are recognizing them and their critically operative posts. We are also consenting to see ourselves being seen, giving consent to being seen. As part of our philosophical formation and life, we should cultivate this intentionality.

Not every gaze is one to which you should grant such authority. Each of us meets gazes of ridicule, shame, belittling, objectification, or indifference. There are those who imagine our destinies falsely—who "fiction make," in Simon's terms. Many people don't even notice us. So we must identify and choose to see the philosophically operative faces. It is in these gazes that we must see ourselves being seen.

Whom Do You See?

In turn, whom do you see? On the back side of your sheet of paper, you might sketch out a stick figure representation of the people that you see in this significant way. For me just now, it is especially my grandchildren. I am especially committed to them because I know from my own experience as a parent just how deeply valuable seeing and being seen by others besides parents has been to my children. I know that parents simply can't do it all on their own. They aren't meant to.

And then you must ask this: Do these others regularly see your face registering your delighted, noticing regard? How may you be more faithful in your philosophical ministrations—in this, your philosophical service?

I should note that we may need to develop some intentionality in composing our faces! When I was young, my mother pointed out to me that I continually scowled. If she called me, whenever I turned round to look at her, I was scowling. It was off-putting. She exhorted me to fix my face! And I do! Thinking of her every time someone behind me calls me, by the time I turn around I have fixed my face to smile welcome. This is important work: our faces particularly are carrying out philosophical formation in the lives of others.

Or we may need to hear a more fundamental admonition: we need to make friends. We make friends by being friends. This is a long, steady covenanting, and one that also proves heaven sent. And friendships must be in person, face to face. They must be characterized by faithfulness and solidarity. These dear people anchor us and sustain us philosophically in our ongoing affirmation and joy in being, and it is our privilege to do the same for them.

In the 2001 film *A Beautiful Mind*, a brilliant but delusional mathematician, John Nash, alongside his wife, receives the psychiatrist's devastating and dismissive diagnosis: "He has no way to tell what is real and what is not." In the quiet of that dark moment of abandonment following the doctor's departure, Nash's wife gently puts her hands on her husband's cheeks, bringing the pair closely face to face. With the quiet authority of love, she speaks: "*This* is real." She sees him. Although he says nothing, it becomes evident that he consents to the authority of her gaze. From that moment, Nash's delusions begin to fade until they no longer speak to him or control him. That is the power of an authoritative, loving, real face in our lives. And it is a deeply philosophical ministration.

9

The Face of God

Our mother's smile and our friends' gazes of noticing regard fail. Mothers, fathers, family, and friends die, or hurt us or abandon us. And even if they could remain blamelessly faithful, the simplest exigencies of life remove them from our sight. Mother must turn her face away to care for your siblings or to cook your dinner. She has to go to work. Although we should be intentional to hang on to them, the dearest of friends move away. Seasons end, and homes are left behind. This brings us to long for a face that will not go away. And it suggests that we are most fully ourselves as we are composed to rest in the gaze of that face.

The Face That Will Not Go Away

According to Hans Urs von Balthasar, Christianity alone fulfills the promise of the mother's smile.[133] This is a stunning assertion. In more technical language, James Loder writes: "The face of the loving parent is prototypical of the Face of God." "In the face-to-face interaction (whether actualized or remaining an innate potential), the child seeks a cosmic, self-confirming impact from the presence of a loving other."[134] The primal experience of Mother's face as actual presence provides a prototype for a person's later experience of the convicting presence of God. In Mother's welcoming smile, Baby's sense of the real begins to be attuned to a reality that is ultimately interpersonal.

Whatever they may think of religion, especially of the Christian religion, people can quite possibly agree to a few things. First, the mother's smile suggests that there is a face that will not go away, and it draws us to long for it. So do the faces of dear friends. Second, the Judeo-Christian Scriptures present the presence of God, Master of the Universe, as that supreme, steadfastly good, true, and beautiful face. True, the thought of the gaze of God might be terrifyingly "in your face"! But for God's people it is a sweet terror, for God's gracious delivering presence composes you in wholeness and freedom. Third, people who consciously reject God nevertheless must be recomposed and anchored in something larger beyond themselves in order to be centered and most fully themselves. And this intimates the Christian story.

Christianity: All About the Face of God

Stepping back and taking the Scriptures as a whole, as many people have done over the centuries, we can see that all of it presents the face of God, intimately, transformatively present, calling us into communion, to live and walk before the gaze of God, with all the attendant blessings (and soberness) of this. It presents the face of God as our highest good.

> The mother's smile suggests that there is a face that will not go away, and it draws us to long for it.

The most famous blessing, the Aaronic Benediction, pronounces that the Lord make his face shine upon us, in grace and peace.[135] As it appears, printed

The Face of God

in uncials, upon the lavender hues of a Welsh landscape watercolor in a framed card I see daily:

> May the Lord bless you and protect you;
> May the Lord's face radiate with Joy because of you;
> May He be gracious to you, show you his favor, and give you his peace.[136]

The psalms enjoin us to seek the Lord's face always; the psalmist writes that seeing the face of God is the one thing to desire above all. Hagar, although an "alien," acknowledges Abraham's God seeing her in rescue and provision and promise, and names God accordingly: *El Roi*, the God who sees me.[137] Significantly for our topic here, the psalmist writes: "When my father and mother forsake me, the LORD will take me up."[138] This God's face is the face that Mother's promises.[139]

The Scriptures overflow with stories of people meeting God because God has come to them and self-revealed. And in the incarnation of Jesus Christ we are given the authoritative image and face of God. On a number of key occasions, Jesus reveals his glory to particular people: to the Magi when they found the Christchild; to the people present at his baptism; to the disciples at the wedding at Cana; to Peter, James, and John in the Transfiguration. "Epiphany" is the word for this self-manifestation, an event in which people's eyes are opened to who he is as he is.[140] There are other face-to-face encounters: the Samaritan woman, Mary Magdalene, Thomas, Peter, and, perhaps most resoundingly, the disciples on the road to Emmaus and the apostle Paul.[141]

In the stories Jesus tells as he teaches, Jesus guides his listeners to see the face of God. Take, for example, the parable of the prodigal son.[142] Imagine the face of that father as he glimpses his besmirched son creeping home, as he hikes up his robes and runs down the road to embrace him! You and I can indwell any of those stories to recognize ourselves as recipients of the gaze of God.

Jesus's name is Emmanuel: God *with* us.[143] The prevailing "motion" of Scripture, according to theologian Michael Williams and others, is the descent of God: God comes to dwell with God's

The Mother's Smile

people.[144] This is the Bible's covenant promise from beginning to end and forever.[145]

A person's event of conversion to be a Christ follower is a redemptive encounter, a being seen transformatively by Christ. It is a seeing oneself being seen by him. Loder's describes the Holy, the fourth dimension of humanness, as "the manifest Presence of being-itself transforming and restoring human being." It recomposes the world. It is a transformational undoing of nothingness, an eruption of new being in the void, supplying the deepest needs of the human being. As we saw, for Loder, a person's experience of the convicting presence of the Lord just is the Face that will not go away.

The psalmist's profession, "When my father and mother forsake me, the LORD will take me up," coincides in good measure with conversion. You recall that I asked my sister, Judy, "Who noticed you?" Her answer had been, "Ohh, Granny Harvey noticed me!" At that time I also asked my Aunt Lorraine, my father's sister, the same question. Her ready reply: "Ohh, Jesus noticed me!" Grandfather Lightcap had died when she was five months old. With her mother and her older brother working to make ends meet, tiny Lorraine was a solitary "latchkey child." At sixteen, however, she heard the good news of Jesus. It opened her eyes and changed her for life. A soprano diva, she became an evangelist, radiating a transforming gaze of beauty as she sang and bore witness to thousands.

For people in the church of Jesus, as with the Emmaus Road disciples, in our gatherings "our eyes are opened in the breaking of the bread."[146] The church's ongoing celebration of the Lord's Supper, the Eucharist, is rightly called Communion. In this sacrament, Jesus welcomes us as guests at his table. The Lord sees us with redemptive delight.

In God's gaze we see God, ourselves, others, and the world, in a new light. "In the Eucharist we are seeing ourselves and our world as they really are, contemplating them in the depths of God, finding their meaning in relation to God," writes Archbishop Rowan Williams.[147]

The Face of God

Christian believers regularly experience the convicting presence of God, brought about by the Holy Spirit, especially by means of reading the Scripture. The Christian life can be seen as living confidently before the gaze of God, beholding God, living forward into the vision of God. All of Scripture and Christianity concerns seeing the face of God.

And can it be that our own rapturous faces bring delight to the Lord in return? According to Scripture, God longs to be known.[148]

Being Seen by God

In my epistemology, I have argued that this redemptive encounter is the foremost paradigm of good knowing.[149] Loder remarks that in the moment of insight active shifts to passive, and the knower is being known. Discovery is a kind of gracious deliverance by the inbreaking real. Granted: it is a lordly paradigm! But my point here is about conversion itself: it involves a transforming being seen, face-to-face with a being beyond ourselves.

In my first identifiable experience of seeing myself being seen in the gaze of a friend, of what I labeled noticing regard, I immediately linked what I was undergoing to Jesus' encounter with the Samaritan woman:[150] "That is just the expression that the woman at the well saw in Jesus' face!" I thought as I noticed my friend's gaze. "He *saw* her! This gaze is what changed her, what redeemed her." My experience inserted me into that story, and I saw the face of the Lord seeing me.

There is so much to mark in this incredibly rich story in John 4. What was a self-respecting young Jewish rabbi doing among Samaria's half-breeds, alone believing he had to travel that way to Galilee? What was he doing talking midday to a woman of questionable repute, asking her for a drink? What of this incredible theological conversation? And what happened?

It is my own surmise that Jesus "had to" go to that place because it was the geographical location and representation of ancient Israel's renewal of the covenant. It was in this place between two

The Mother's Smile

mountains, Gerizim and Ebal, that the Mosaic covenant had been renewed by Joshua as the Israelite people entered the land God had given them. In this natural amphitheater, one group of people had stood on verdant Gerizim and pronounced the covenant's blessings; the other group had pronounced its curses from the heights of barren Ebal. Jacob's well at their base gave forth "living water" which flowed from the springs beneath lush Gerizim. Jesus sat down on that well, I surmise, identifying himself authoritatively as himself the final renewal of the covenant, himself the living water.

In the terms of the older covenant, that woman was unforgiveable, unsavable. But here was Jesus, the quintessential seventh Bridegroom, and in his face she saw him seeing her. It was noticing regard, as I was experiencing in that moment with my friend, but it was qualitatively more: it was unprecedented, old-law abrogating, authoritative, redemptive absolution. Jesus was naming her unforgivable status in the act of ridding her of it in the new covenant in his very body. Her response clearly indicated her transformation and liberation, her dawning understanding: she ran to bring her (likewise unforgiveable) enemies to meet Jesus.

From another Gospel event we can glimpse the transformative recomposing that the face of the Lord brings about: the worst-ever afflicted demon possessed man ran wild among the graves on the southern bank of the Galilee Sea. Jesus faced off with the legion of demons possessing him. He rid the man of them, allowing them to enter a herd of pigs nearby. The pigs plunged wildly down to their destruction in the lake. When nearby folk ran to the scene, no doubt angry about their pigs (Wait—pigs?), they were astounded—actually, terrified—to find the man "clothed, and in his right mind, sitting at Jesus' feet."[151] In Jesus' liberating gaze, the man was fundamentally recomposed.

To relate the amazing story of Emmaus: a couple of distraught disciples journeyed from Jerusalem to Emmaus in the wake of Jesus's horrific crucifixion, which had dashed their recent hopes for the Messiah.[152] A young rabbi joined them, and curiously didn't seem to share their horror. Then he started exhorting them about the Scriptures' promise. The disciples failed to recognize him (although their bodies seemed to have been doing so—their hearts had been burning) until later; they took their eyes off his face to watch his blessing and breaking of bread. Only then were their eyes opened to see his face, to recognize that it was Jesus, once dead, now having triumphed over death. Once again, exuberantly transformed action ensued. This resurrection changed the entire world.

Finally, consider the astounding story of the woman who anointed Jesus with a costly jar of perfume. In this we see the impact of having been seen by Jesus. This text overflows with cultural improprieties, according to Middle-Eastern-culture expert Kenneth Bailey.[153] Jesus's "host" blatantly ignored the most basic honor due to a guest—anointing his head with oil and washing and toweling his feet. Then Jesus nevertheless blatantly reclined at the table, perhaps drawing a provocative line in the sand. With a showdown brewing, a social reject present (a custom of the time), a woman deemed unclean, took it upon herself to atone for the host's rudeness by anointing Jesus' feet with her costly perfume and her tears, using her hair in place of the unprovided towel. And Jesus not only let her touch him, flagrantly violating social taboos, but scandalously he also spoke to her directly. He spoke about her to his host to criticize his host's offenses, to affirm that the woman alone grasped the truth of the situation—the inevitability of his impending sacrifice. Jesus honored her act as one of beauty, ever to be told and remembered. This woman's having been seen redemptively by Jesus had recomposed her. She saw herself being seen by the Lord, and therein forgiven and set free. This seeing issued in a heroic act of solidarity with the Lord in moments of his own deepening need.

To deepen our grasp of the enormity of what each of these women and men has experienced in their encounter with the Lord, we may imagine each responding in the words of Psalm 116. Being seen by the Lord, and being saved, are effectively the same thing.

> I love the LORD, for he heard my voice;
>   he heard my cry for mercy.
> The cords of death entangled me, the anguish of the grave came upon me;

The Mother's Smile

> I was overcome by trouble and sorrow.
> Then I called on the name of the Lord: "O Lord, save me!"
> The Lord is gracious and righteous;
>   our God is full of compassion.
> The Lord protects the simplehearted;
>   when I was in great need, he saved me.
> You, O Lord, have delivered my soul from death,
>   my eyes from tears,
>   my feet from stumbling,
> that I may walk before the Lord in the land of the living.
> How can I repay the Lord for all his goodness to me?
> O Lord, truly I am your servant;
>   I am your servant, the child of your maidservant;
>   you have freed me from my chains.
> I will sacrifice a thank offering to you;
> I will fulfill my vows to the Lord
>   in the presence of all his people,
> in the courts of the house of the Lord—
>   in your midst, O Jerusalem.
> Praise the Lord.

To be seen by God is to be delivered and liberated, to be made over fresh and whole, to be trophies of grace and beauty and courage and peace. It is to be welcomed to belong in an inbreaking, new world. Of course, this side of the end of all things, we both know and don't yet know his gaze. We have been redeemed, and we walk before his face (*coram Deo*); but also we await his promised, culminating, coming. We still long for the final appearing of the face that will never go away—for the culminating fulfillment of the promise of the mother's smile. Seeing the face of God is the beatific vision, the most blessed thing. Those who long for and see the face of God find that Mother's and all other operative faces have been pointing to his.

The Face of God

The (Not Ultimate, but) Proximate Primacy of Fleshly Faces

Believers seeking to exalt the face of Christ can be tempted to downplay the faces of human persons. Sometimes people even discredit the import of others' noticing regard and their own notice of it, deeming it only pride and vanity, sinful idolatry. Believers can think it spiritually superior to presume that the face of the Lord should be the only face we need. I believe that the Scripture itself says, yes, the Lord's face is enough, but that this is actually an unnatural, situation. "When my mother and my father forsake me": that's not the plan but the extreme exception. It's not either-or; it's both-and. It's from-to. It's the *from* that anticipatively attunes us to the *to*, the *to* that finally fully makes sense of the *from*. Childbirth, God's own bringing persons into existence, has installed a natural (primal, not final) primacy of the human face. For every single human person the world over, it is the mother's smile, which under ordinary circumstances they are born into, whose promise Christianity alone fulfills. That's one reason why, in this book, I have accented the faces of humans and other things. This little book exists to call attention to and confer dignity on the creaturely faces who notice us in delighted regard.

Let us not overlook the glorious distinctive of the Christian religion: There was a time in the history of our world that people saw the very human face of God himself. This is the wonder of the incarnation of Jesus, the second person of the Holy Trinity. When I saw the noticing regard of my friend, I saw the human face of the Lord Jesus Christ as seen by the Samaritan woman. But this profound point displays how the incarnation roundly affirms the value and dignity of creation, including of the everyday faces who see me with regard. Thus it supports my claim here.[154]

Truth to tell, it's been the human faces in my life who revised my misperception of the face of God. I spent the earlier decades of my life mistakenly imagining God's facial visage toward me as wearing a displeased, disapproving, shaming, critical look—or at its best, a countenance of patient toleration! Surely a key experience

The Mother's Smile

of the Holy in my life has been fixing this misperception, as in the face of a friend I recognized the gaze the Samaritan woman saw, in a human face regarding me.

We do need human faces; we certainly need mothers and friends. We need them for our philosophical formation. We need them to promise and to orient us to the face of God. Created and divine faces are profoundly connected: we commonly associate the aphorism, "To love another person is to see the face of God" with Victor Hugo's moving novel, *Les Miserables*. And I would add:—and to be the face of God to another.

From our birth into our mother's welcoming smile, and in the sustaining gaze of dear family and friends, we are formed philosophically to orient to the face that will not go away: in our sense of our own existence, in our knowing ventures and all our involvement with the real. And in reality itself, we implicitly seek the face of God as the most real thing.

10

Delight

Your Philosophical Service

As I have been writing this book, I have been watching my daughter, Starr, with her new baby, Laurence. Their face-to-face time is constant just now! She holds and nurses Laurie in steady welcome. I have been watching the rapturous faces of Laurie's dad and siblings. I have been beaming my own delight at him as his nearby Grandmamà. I am seeing Laurie see back and start to smile and gurgle in conversation. He is seeing himself being seen. He is recognizing being recognized. He is responding to being addressed; and in little summoning "barks" he is now addressing. His smile is radiant, and he is becoming exuberant about things! I write this book to say that this natal welcome is forming Laurie philosophically.

Summing Up

The Mother's Smile has been making a philosophical claim: that the smiling encounter of Mother and friends is key to our philosophical formation. Our mothers, families, and friends carry out

The Mother's Smile

fundamental philosophy, equipping us and sustaining us in our ever-philosophical life.

In this intimate, dynamic interpersonal encounter and communion our sense of our own astonishing existence comes to be. We are shaped in our natural fundamental orientation of a joyous *yes* to reality. We receive and participate in this paradigm in all our best involvement with the world in our knowing and making—the ideal of face-to-face encounter and ongoing conviviality. The encounter of Mother and child attunes us to the real's welcome, and to the brimming overflow of things self-showing, self-giving, self-saying, offering themselves in relationship and noble service. We are formed to commune with things as others—others the same as me, different from me, related to me, due my noticing regard. We sense the promise of the mother's smile: the hope of the face of God that will not go away. This is the philosophical fruit of the mother's smile.

I've argued also that primal welcome unfolds into a healthy philosophy, truer to ourselves and to the rest of reality than have been the defective philosophical presumptions that define modernism. I've called us to return to this philosophy of childhood, and in so doing subverting and dispelling the modernist paradigm we may have imbibed as we grew older. And I've suggested that our reflection together here can heighten our intentionality in living in philosophical awareness—in reclaiming what is our philosophical birthright as human persons. To be human is to be lovers of

> **It may well be that you, right now, are Mother. Be affirmed in this, your strategic and profound philosophical ministration. Be as intentional to delight in your little one as you have the strength and grace to be.**

Delight

the real, to be made for encounter and communion with it. Thus, Schindler: philosophy is an all-encompassing love of the real, a love only deepened by Christian faith.

Your Philosophical Service: Delight

A main takeaway of this book's proposal: in addition to consenting to being seen, you should practice seeing. You should enact welcoming regard.

It may well be that you, right now, are Mother—the one of whom we have been speaking centrally in this book! From your *en face* in your wonder-filled birthing, through countless hours of nursing, humbling faithful care, careful watching as your child plays, wording their world and welcoming it together, you get to be the very one in whose rapturous gaze of welcome your child is being formed philosophically. Be affirmed in this, your strategic and profound philosophical ministration. Be as intentional to delight in your little one as you have the strength and grace to be.

I believe that parents' most important task with their children is to delight in them: steady, noticing regard. Be intentional to resist looking elsewhere unnecessarily in their presence, for example at your phone. Make your face light up, not with the sepulchral light of a device, but with the light of your countenance. Also, prudently involve your children with others who will see them, too: your family, your special friends, your pets and yard and town and things. Bring your children with you to the Lord's table of welcome.

Friends, perform your distinctive philosophical ministration: be the face of noticing regard for those linked to you in special solidarity. Make it so that the significant others in your life see your face registering delight and regard as you gaze at them. Listen so well to these friends that you can imagine their destinies truly. Be gratified to understand your sustained philosophical service.

Even if it doesn't at first feel natural to offer a countenance of delighted regard, pretend, fake it, until it is natural! We tend to think faking it is shallow because artificial. I'd like to suggest that you have to work at certain things in order to restore them to their

The Mother's Smile

natural condition. This is entirely legitimate and worthwhile. In our lives, a smile is primal, we have reason to affirm.

Pocket your cell phone in the presence of your dearest others. Turn away (and turn them away) from TV or phone to see them steadily. The operative faces in your life cannot be merely virtual. Nor can your face convey noticing regard—nor can you even see others in encounter—only virtually. For one thing, in virtual conversations on our screens our eyes can't even look directly into each other's eyes.

Smiling presupposes looking at someone directly in the eyes. In our modern age, sadly we are losing this fundamental propriety. Resist this attrition in your dealings in life. Anyone will find that smiling itself brings oneself delight, integration, and wholeness. For encounter is mutual. Smiling is primal philosophy: it is wonder sustained.

Do not reserve your smile only for your significant others. Smile courteously at the person passing you in the street, the one checking you and your groceries out at the store, (in New Jersey) the person who pumps your gas. It's hard to resist a smile. Your smile may be just what they need. It is key, for example, in the film, *Thirteen Conversations About One Thing*: a smile prevents a suicide. A countenance of welcome changes the course of a life and a world.

Do not forget to make your face shine not only on persons but on the places and things in your care and inquiry, on your neighborhood, your city, your work, your world. "The world needs a cosmic Yes to be spoken to it." It needs to be seen to grow more fully into itself. It is due our attention, our noticing regard, our "So! It is You!" Practicing noticing regard is your privileged philosophical service in the world. You may need to remove your headphones and earbuds to listen and say yes to the world.

Thanks and Other Takeaways

Here are other implications of what we have been saying here. First, thank and honor your mother. Thank her for being your first philosophy professor, the one who opened an ontological paradise

Delight

to you and welcomed you, in wonder and astonishment, to belong in it. Thank her for the long and sacrificial humility of her giving herself to you in intimate encounter, therein enacting and modeling the best-ever epistemology and metaphysics. Thank her for seeing you and allowing you to see yourself being seen in delight and regard.

You may well be like I have been: I have needed to address my own seeing. I have needed to see myself being seen. Once I identified it and felt it, I found that being seen was retroactive: it was a seeing that carried back to my birth as well as beyond to God. I have had to resolve to override the acedic *no* that blinded my eyes to the regard of others. I have spoken of my feeling unnoticed. I now believe that I may have been guilty of resistance: I'm told that my English Granny Harvey pronounced about baby me, "This child will not be nursed!" I presume that means that I did not acquiesce to be comforted by holding, caring presence. Big on seeing things, not so big on seeing myself being seen. Despite this, I admit humbly, despite the difficulty that this late-born surprise baby brought into her life, despite the distractions of a difficult life of her own, despite the expectations normative for her heritage and time period, despite my own appalling adolescent ambivalence to her, my mother watched and nurtured me as faithfully and generously as she could. My subsequent experience as a mother grew me in appreciation of her necessary sacrifice. And as I say, the faces of other friends over the years, and my own humbling (philosophical) realization, have enlarged my estimate of her. I note particularly that my mother was a thoughtful teacher and writer, which I aspire to be. And my mother read to me—a lot. Thank you, Mother!

So, second, you yourself, be healed! Sometimes we must be enjoined to see—to see the face of the other seeing us. It takes a kind of consent to see oneself being seen. Consent is irresistible for the loved and cradled child. The hardships of subsequent years can make this consent more difficult further along in our lives. And that includes the hardship of implicit modernist philosophy, which, among its many other acedic faults, doesn't even acknowledge the

The Mother's Smile

very role of responsible consent in knowing. On the other hand, it is likely that delighted regard of Mother and friends persists through hardship: readers of *Harry Potter* understand that it was the love of Harry's mother, who sacrificed her life to save him as a baby, that remains key to his overcoming the horrific adversity he faces again and again.[155]

For all of us, throughout our lives, third, we must identify the select few faces of friends and family who see us with steady, noticing regard. Whose are the operative faces in your life? Whose gaze, as it lights on you, beams with delighted regard? In whose gaze can you see yourself being seen, trusting that vision of you? In whose gaze do you grow to be more yourself? On the other hand, whose faces of indifference or belittling must you ignore?

For this Grandmamà, just now the joyous faces who see me are my grandchildren's. Applying in all sincerity the well-known quip about our dogs: may I be the person they think I am! A few other family members and friends perform this service in my life. Two important ones whom I don't now see in person I nevertheless see gazing at me from picture frames as I work. I live out their earlier unwavering estimate of me. And for me as an author and speaker, you readers and all who listen and respond also see me in my particular form of communion with the real. You minister philosophically, conferring "hereness" and dignity, confirming that communion is the paradigm of knowing, that reality invites and welcomes, allowing glimpses of the face of the prodigal (extravagantly generous) God.

So, fourth, thank those friends who have seen you and who continue to see you with delight and welcome. Count them dear and keep these friendships. Undoubtedly there have been faces who have seen you: you are at this very moment reflecting philosophically out of a competency and interest sufficient for our conversation together. Even if your upbringing has been tragic, if you are reading this, somewhere there have been and are such gazes, or their absence has formed you in hope for one such which will not go away. Live out steady awareness of and gratitude for this your

Delight

philosophical formation in the welcoming smile of your mother and friends.

You readers and hearers are a particular sort of operative friends and face for me in my work, and so I thank you for this philosophical service rendered to me. I continue to see you seeing me, responding to me, maturing me and my thought toward wholeness. I say it here, and I say it as I have occasion to connect directly with you.

Perish the thought: there are no such faces in your life. I believe that this is a well-nigh impossible negative extreme. But it may be that your dearest operative face or faces have betrayed or left you. Even this wretched absence, in its absence, points to a face that will not go away. So, fifth, seek this face, the face of God. Cry out for it. "When my father and my mother forsake me, the LORD will take me up" (Ps 27:10), Scripture promises. This is a matter of hope and grace.

Living before the face of God may require an intentional reversal in your outlook from the all-too-common presumption of a divine countenance of shaming wrath and condemnation. Counter this with determined resolve to seek God's face, as the psalmist enjoins; counter it by imagining, for example, the face of the father of the prodigal son in Jesus' story. Be attentive: expect humbly that the God you want to know won't turn down the invitation! Re-envision this real world as one in which the Lord comes. God saw and sees us into existence, in every moment, in every atom—here, now; here, now, in this lively real. See the world as his can't-help-himself overflow of love, self-showing, self-giving, and self-saying. God comes in the incarnation of Jesus Christ. God sees us into redemption. God welcomes us into communion. Seek to be steadily with the gathered church, especially at the Lord's table of welcome. God shows up in experiences of his convicting presence. God comes in his Word. The Lord Jesus promises his return.

Finally, allow this fundamental encounter, mother's and others', to play out philosophically. Realize and cultivate your philosophical life. Be intentional to restore and embrace your natural natal philosophy, which rightly challenges and even dispels modernity's prevailing but disorienting mindset; embrace your deepest sense of your involvement with things, which operates even when we attempt inconsistently to falsify it.

Never get over the astonishment and belonging that began with your primal encounter. Persistently recur to the wonder of your existence. Along with Chesterton, ask, "Can I thank no one for the birthday present of birth?" How may you, as he also asks, contrive to be at once astonished at the world and at home in it? Be intentional to enact a fundamental orientation of affirmation and joy in being.

How may you be what you were meant to be: a lover of the real, in lively communion with it? Return to your natural metaphysics of childhood in your lived sense of reality. Be intentional to notice things with delight, and to anticipate that they will respond to your countenance. Remember Capon's trenchant aphorism: "The world needs all the lovers—amateurs—it can get."

Retrain the way you see reality: things are astonishingly existing coherent unities brimming with splendid more, offering themselves in personal relatedness, in beauty, goodness and truth to the end of communion. Bring to the real things of the world your face of delighted noticing regard.

Practice an epistemology of welcome: Let delighted notice and attention begin your knowing ventures. Love in order to know. Reciprocate the real's noble courtesy. Look for discovery and insight to have the shape of mutual encounter to the end of intimate communion. Exercise the regard due to others, human and non-human. Seek and behold the face of God seeing you, our highest happiness. To this enveloping communion all these everyday philosophical enactments bear witness. In all these ways live from your philosophical formation in the welcoming smile of your mother and friends, and into its promise.

Endnotes

1. Percy, "Naming and Being," 133.
2. Polanyi, *Personal Knowledge*. For a concise summary of Polanyi's philosophical contribution, see Grene, "Tacit Knowing."
3. Meek, *Contact with Reality*.
4. Meek, *Longing to Know*.
5. Meek, *Contact with Reality*, chap. 5.
6. Meek, *Longing to Know*, 207.
7. Meek, *Loving to Know*.
8. Meek, *Little Manual for Knowing*.
9. Schindler, *Catholicity of Reason*, chap. 2 ("Surprised by Truth").
10. Balthasar, "Movement Toward God," 15.
11. Schindler, *Catholicity of Reason*, 45.
12. Meek, *Doorway to Artistry*.
13. Descartes, *Meditations*, 24.
14. Wittgenstein, *Philosophical Investigations*, 115.
15. Trevathan, "Maternal 'En Face.'"
16. Loder, *Transforming Moment*, 162–63.
17. Meek, *Loving to Know*, chap. 7.
18. Other philosophical matters that could well be considered in themselves include language and ethics: I leave reflection on these to you and others.
19. Kimmerer, *Braiding Sweetgrass*, 26.
20. Buber, *I and Thou*, 51 and throughout.
21. Loder, *Transforming* Moment, chap. 3.
22. Robinson, *Gilead*, 52–53.
23. Meek, *Loving to Know*, chap. 8, and texture 6.

Endnotes

24. Spaemann, *Spaemann Reader*, 83, 85.
25. Rowling, *Harry Potter*, chap. 12.
26. Spaemann, *Spaemann Reader*, 81, 92–93.
27. Moltmann-Wendell, *I Am My Body*, 104.
28. Spaemann, *Spaemann Reader*, 81.
29. Spaemann, *Spaemann Reader*, 83.
30. One playful instance comes to mind: occasionally shorthand would appear on the kitchen blackboard, probably concerning gifts—my parents were communicating about me!
31. Spaemann, *Spaemann Reader*, 92–93.
32. Spaemann, *Spaemann Reader*, 81.
33. Spaemann, *Spaemann Reader*, 82.
34. Spaemann, *Spaemann Reader*, 84.
35. Spaemann, *Spaemann Reader*, 89.
36. I call it an anti-philosophy because modernism disavows philosophy itself in deference to its ideal of utility. A philosophy that denies that it itself is a philosophy is obviously problematic.
37. Spaemann, *Spaemann Reader*, 82.
38. Meek, *Loving to Know*, chap. 2.
39. Macmurray, *Persons in Relation*, 24; Meek, *Loving to Know*, chap. 8.
40. Macmurray, *Persons in Relation*, 228.
41. Schindler, *Love and the Postmodern Predicament*, chap. 4.
42. Schindler, *Catholicity of Reason*, 45.
43. Schindler, *Catholicity of Reason*, 259.
44. Spaemann, *Spaemann Reader*, 82.
45. Spaemann, *Spaemann Reader*, 222.
46. Spaemann, *Spaemann Reader*, 222.
47. Spaemann, *Spaemann Reader*, 94.
48. Schindler, *Love and the Postmodern Predicament*, chap. 2.
49. Schindler, *Catholicity of Reason*, 259–60.
50. Schindler, *Catholicity of Reason*, 45.
51. Schindler, *Plato's Critique of Impure Reason*, chap. 3: "Breaking In: Reversal and Reality, Or, How Socrates as the Real Image of the Good, fulfills the Sun, the Line, and the Cave Images by Overturning Them."
52. Spaemann, *Spaemann Reader*, 95.
53. Schindler, *Catholicity of Reason*, 11.
54. Schindler, *Catholicity of Reason*, 9.
55. Meek, *Doorway to Artistry*, chap. 6.
56. Schindler, *Catholicity of Reason*, 18.
57. Schindler, *Catholicity of Reason*, 18.
58. Schindler, *Catholicity of Reason*, chap. 4.

Endnotes

59. Schindler, *Catholicity of Reason*, 259.
60. Schindler, *Catholicity of Reason*, 253.
61. Schindler, *Catholicity of Reason*, 113.
62. Schindler, *Catholicity of Reason*, 113.
63. Schindler, *Catholicity of Reason*, 259.
64. Meek, *Loving to Know*, chap. 15.
65. Meek, *Doorway to Artistry*.
66. Schindler, *Catholicity of Reason*, 9.
67. Schindler, *Love and the Postmodern Predicament*, 3.
68. Schindler, *Catholicity of Reason*, 12.
69. Hart, *Beauty of the Infinite*, 253.
70. Schindler, *Catholicity of Reason*, chap. 1.
71. Polanyi, *Personal Knowledge*, vii, 55–56.
72. Quoted in Schindler, *Catholicity of Reason*, 47.
73. Schindler, *Catholicity of Reason*, 49–50.
74. Buber, *I and Thou*, 116–17.
75. Schindler, *Catholicity of Reason*, 56.
76. Schindler, *Catholicity of Reason*, 45, 49.
77. Balthasar, Movement Toward God," 15–17.
78. Schindler, *Catholicity of Reason*, 46–47.
79. Marohn, *Tuttle*.
80. Chesterton, *Everlasting Man*, 14.
81. Quoted in Schindler, *Catholicity of Reason*, 12.
82. Spaemann, *A Robert Spaemann Reader*, 90.
83. Chesterton, *Orthodoxy*, 9.
84. Pieper, *Leisure the Basis of Culture*, 43–46.
85. Spaemann, *Spaemann Reader*, 81–82.
86. Spaemann, *Spaemann Reader*, 83–85.
87. Spaemann, *Spaemann Reader*, 92.
88. Spaemann, *Spaemann Reader*, 81.
89. Spaemann, *Spaemann Reader*, 81.
90. Spaemann, *Spaemann Reader*, 222.
91. Spaemann, *Spaemann Reader*, 91.
92. Spaemann, *Spaemann Reader*, 85.
93. Spaemann, *Spaemann Reader*, 87.
94. Spaemann, *Spaemann Reader*, 86.
95. Spaemann, *Spaemann Reader*, 86.
96. Spaemann, *Spaemann Reader*, 88.
97. Spaemann, *Spaemann Reader*, 91.
98. Spaemann, *Spaemann Reader*, 88.

Endnotes

99. Meek, *Doorway to Artistry*, chap. 4.
100. Clarke, "Introduction," xv–xvi.
101. Hanby, *No God? No Science?*, 347. Hanby attributes the term to Adrian Walker.
102. Schindler, *Catholicity of Reason*, 65–67.
103. Williams, *Grace and Necessity*, 138–40.
104. Meek, *Contact with Reality*.
105. Schindler, *Catholicity of Reason*, 64.
106. Meek, *Doorway to Artistry*, chap. 4.
107. Hanby, *No God? No Science?*, chap. 2.
108. Chesterton, *Orthodoxy*, 49.
109. Chesterton, *Orthodoxy*, 54–55.
110. Chesterton, *Orthodoxy*, 53–54.
111. Capon, *Supper of the Lamb*, 19.
112. Capon, *Supper of the Lamb*, chap. 2.
113. Schindler, *Love and the Postmodern Predicament*, 26.
114. Schindler, *Love and the Postmodern Predicament*, 76.
115. Schindler, *Ulrich's* Homo Abyssus, 189.
116. Schindler, *Ulrich's* Homo Abyssus, 77.
117. Capon, *Supper of the Lamb*, 3–5.
118. Schindler, *Love and the Postmodern Predicament*, 3. In "all-encompassing," the reader can also hear the notes of the primacy of the whole—the irreducible face of things.
119. Schindler, *Catholicity of Reason*, 45.
120. Schindler, *Catholicity of Reason*, 56.
121. Macmurray, *Persons in Relation*, 228.
122. Macmurray, *Persons in Relation*, 61.
123. Meek, *Doorway to Artistry*, chap. 8 ("Feast").
124. Kimmerer, *Braiding Sweetgrass*.
125. Kimmerer, *Braiding Sweetgrass*, 345–46.
126. Kimmerer, *Braiding Sweetgrass*, 56. Kimmerer draws this quotation from Thomas Berry.
127. Kimmerer, *Braiding Sweetgrass*, 167–204.
128. Kimmerer, *Braiding Sweetgrass*, 36–38.
129. Kimmerer, *Braiding Sweetgrass*, 48–62.
130. Kimmerer, *Braiding Sweetgrass*, 205–15.
131. Moltmann-Wendel, *I Am My Body*, 10–11.
132. Simon, *The Disciplined Heart*.
133. Balthasar, "Movement Toward God," 15–17.
134. Loder, *Transforming Moment*, 163.

Endnotes

135. Numbers 6:22–27.
136. Notably, a dear friend sent this card on the occasion of my sister Judy's passing.
137. Genesis 16:13.
138. Psalm 27:10 (KJV).
139. It can be a matter of terror to see the face of God, the Scriptures suggest. As you may imagine, a person might not want to see God's face if they have been up to no good. And it can sometimes seem as if in our suffering God might be paying too much attention: the Psalmist cries, "Look away from me, that I may enjoy life again, before I depart and am no more" (Psalm 39:13). We need only recall that God is no ordinary person. His face would not be merely blandly sweet. (Neither was our mother's!) Our lives lie entirely in his consent, goodness, power, justice, and mercy. Hence the need for that benediction: "may the LORD lift his countenance upon you."
140. These events are marked out for the Sundays in Epiphany in the Episcopal *Book of Common Prayer*.
141. John 4; John 20; John 20; John 21; Luke 24; Acts 9.
142. Luke 15.
143. Matthew 1:23.
144. Meek, *Loving to Know*, 200.
145. Revelation 21:3.
146. Luke 24:30–31.
147. Williams, *Being Christian*, 59.
148. Acts 17:24–28.
149. Meek, *Loving to Know*.
150. John 4.
151. Luke 8:35.
152. Luke 24.
153. Bailey, *Jesus Through Middle Eastern Eyes*, chap. 18.
154. As Michael Hanby reports, it is the incarnation that leads to the fresh version of the doctrine of creation expressed in John 1. (Hanby, "A Brief History of the Cosmos," chap. 2 in *No God? No Science?*) Thanks to my editor, Dr. Robin Parry, for contributing this important insight.
155. Rowling, *Harry Potter and the Sorcerer's Stone*, chap. 17.

Bibliography

Aquinas, Thomas. *De Veritate*. https://aquinas.cc/la/en/~QDeVer.Q1.9.
Bailey, Kenneth E. *Jesus Through Middle Eastern Eyes: Cultural Studies in the Gospels*. Downers Grove, IL: IVP Academic, 2008.
Balthasar, Hans Urs von. "Movement Toward God." In *Explorations in Theology III: Creator Spirit*, translated by Brian McNeil, 15–56. San Francisco: Ignatius, 1967.
Buber, Martin. *I and Thou*. Translated by Walter Kaufmann. New York: Scribner's Sons, 1970.
Capon, Robert Farrar. *The Supper of the Lamb: A Culinary Reflection*. New York: Harcourt Brace Jovanovitch, 1969.
Chesterton, G. K. *The Everlasting Man*. 1925. Reprint, San Francisco: Ignatius, 1993.
———. *Orthodoxy: The Romance of Faith*. 1908. Reprint, New York: Doubleday, 1990.
Clarke, W. Norris. "Introduction." In *An Introduction to the Metaphysics of St. Thomas Aquinas*, translated and edited by James F. Anderson, ix–xxii. Washington, DC: Regnery, 1997.
———. *The One and the Many: A Contemporary Thomistic Metaphysics*. Notre Dame: Notre Dame University Press, 2001.
Descartes, Rene. *Meditations on First Philosophy*. Translated by Laurence J. Lafleur. Indianapolis: Bobbs-Merrill, 1960.
Grene, Marjorie. "Tacit Knowing: Grounds for a Revolution in Philosophy." *Journal of the British Society for Phenomenology* 8 (1977) 164–71.
Hanby, Michael. *No God? No Science? Theology, Cosmology, Biology*. Oxford: Wiley-Blackwell, 2013.
Hart, David Bentley. *The Beauty of the Infinite: The Aesthetics of Christian Truth*. Grand Rapids: Eerdmans, 2003.
Kimmerer, Robin Wall. *Braiding Sweetgrass: Indigenous Wisdom, Scientific Knowledge, and the Teachings of Plants*. Minneapolis: Milkweed, 2013.

Bibliography

Loder, James. *The Transforming Moment*. 2nd ed. Colorado Springs: Helmers and Howard, 1989.

Macmurray, John. *Persons in Relation*. Atlantic Highlands, NJ: Humanities, 1991.

Meek, Esther Lightcap. *Contact with Reality: Michael Polanyi's Realism and Why It Matters*. Eugene, OR: Cascade, 2017.

———. *Doorway to Artistry: Attuning Your Philosophy to Enhance Your Creativity*. Eugene, OR: Cascade, 2023.

———. *A Little Manual for Knowing*. Eugene, OR: Cascade, 2014.

———. *Longing to Know: The Philosophy of Knowledge for Ordinary People*. Grand Rapids: Brazos, 2003.

———. *Loving to Know: Introducing Covenant Epistemology*. Eugene, OR: Cascade, 2011.

Marohn, Nancy. *Tuttle*. Pictures by Harper Landell. Philadelphia: Winston, 1949.

Moltmann-Wendel, Elisabeth. *I Am My Body: A Theology of Embodiment*. New York: Continuum, 1995.

Percy, Walker. "Naming and Being." In *Signposts in a Strange Land*, 131–38. New York: Farrar, Straus, and Giroux, 1991.

Pieper, Josef. *Leisure: The Basis of Culture*. San Francisco: Ignatius, 2009.

Polanyi, Michael. *Personal Knowledge: Towards a Post-Critical Philosophy*. Chicago: University of Chicago Press, 1958, 1962.

Robinson, Marilynne. *Gilead*. New York: Macmillan, 2006.

Rowling, J. K. *Harry Potter and the Sorcerer's Stone*. New York: Levine, 1998.

Schindler, D. C. *The Catholicity of Reason*. Grand Rapids: Eerdmans, 2013.

———. *A Companion to Ferdinand Ulrich's* Homo Abyssus. Baltimore: Humanum Academic, 2019.

———. *Love and the Postmodern Predicament: Rediscovering the Real in Beauty, Goodness, and Truth*. Veritas. Eugene, OR: Cascade, 2017.

———. *Plato's Critique of Impure Reason: On Goodness and Truth in* The Republic. Washington, DC: Catholic University of America Press, 2008.

Simon, Caroline. *The Disciplined Heart: Love, Destiny, and Imagination*. Grand Rapids: Eerdmans, 1997.

Spaemann, Robert. *A Robert Spaemann Reader: Philosophical Essays on Nature, God, and the Human Person*. Edited and translated by D. C. Schindler and Jeanne Heffernan Schindler. Oxford: Oxford University Press, 2015.

Trevathan, W. R. "Maternal 'En Face' Orientation During the First Hour After Birth." *The American Journal of Orthopsychiatry* 53.1 (1983) 92–99.

Williams, Rowan. *Being Christian: Baptism, Bible, Eucharist, Prayer*. Grand Rapids: Eerdmans, 2014.

———. *Grace and Necessity: Reflections on Art and Love*. Harrisburg, PA: Morehouse, 2005.

Wittgenstein, Ludwig. *Philosophical Investigations*. 3rd ed. New York: Macmillan, 1958.

www.ingramcontent.com/pod-product-compliance
Lightning Source LLC
Chambersburg PA
CBHW031349160426
43196CB00007B/788